STRATEGIC DIVESTMENT

STRATEGIC DIVESTMENT

Leonard Vignola, Jr.

A DIVISION OF AMERICAN MANAGEMENT ASSOCIATIONS

© 1974 AMACOM
A division of American Management Associations, New York. All rights
reserved. Printed in the United States of America.

International standard book number: 0-8144-5347-3

Library of Congress catalog card number: 73-85193

First printing

Preface

THE PURPOSE OF THIS BOOK is to examine the art of letting go. Divestment is considered entirely within the context of the business community and solely as a business undertaking. The intent is to analyze both its theoretical and its practical structure: its motivations and objectives; the problems it involves, its advantages and disadvantages, and its mechanics and procedures. Case histories are used extensively to illustrate its various aspects.

To divest primarily means to strip of clothing, ornament, or equipment. From that arises its use in business: to deprive or dispossess, especially of property, authority, or title. This definition of the word emphasizes the purposes of this book—to investigate the dispossessing, ridding, or freeing of businesses, products, plants, distribution facilities, and various other assets owned by companies.

However, definition is as much what it is not as what it is. Divesting, as considered in this book, is neither the sale of the entire company nor the shutting down or closing of all or a portion of a company. The discussion of divesting has been limited to situations in which only part but not all of the firm's activities are divested. Following the divestment, the divesting company continues as a distinct, viable business entity. In fact, if the divestment is planned and implemented effectively, the divesting company realizes certain benefits or advantages that strengthen it as an operating unit. As for shutting down, discontinuing, or terminating a plant, product line, or other company activity, the action can be a response to the same set of problems or causes that might prompt divestment but is separate and distinct from a divestment. Accordingly, closing or shutting down is mentioned only in a general way as an alternative to divestment. One other point in connection with the definition of divestment should be noted. Divestment will be considered as a process or procedure and not simply as an isolated and discrete act.

The frequency of divestment occurrences has accelerated quite rapidly since the late 1960s, and Chapter 1 supplies the available statistics on divestment activity. To divest is a key management decision, and divestment is viewed in that light in Chapters 2 to 4. Those chapters deal with the objectives of divestment, the determination that a situation warrants divestment consideration, and the alternatives to divestment that must be examined. It bears repeating that divestment is not an isolated decision or occurrence but is instead part and parcel of a management decision-making process.

Diverting is also a procedure. A company must prepare for a divestment; it must select and contact prospective purchasers, and it must develop and negotiate the divestment transaction or package. Those topics are the subject of Chapters 5 to 9. Finally, a critical aspect of the success of any divestment is implementation. Chapters 10 to 12 touch on the implementation, particularly as it affects employee, customer, supplier, and community relations.

The book is intended to be a discussion of divestment useful to those who are directly involved in the divestment decision—the chairman, president, key vice presidents, financial officer, and major division and department heads—and also those who assist or advise management on divestment decisions from both within and without companies—planning personnel, accountants, consultants, bankers, and lawyers. It is designed to facilitate thinking and to broaden the approach to divesting, particularly as an important course of action open to a firm in certain situations. It has not been written as either a textbook or a guide to specific details or precise technical or procedural points.

Throughout, the book reflects my thinking and my personal experience with divesting in the course of my own business career. In several of the chapters, I express decided views on various phases of the divestment process. However, I have also included data from secondary sources on divestment frequency and examples that illustrate or emphasize certain characteristics of divestments. The results of a survey on corporate divestment mailed to over two hundred American companies are interspersed to develop certain points about divesting.

I am indebted to the American Management Associations and, particularly, Ernest Miller for their confidence and infinite patience. Also, I am grateful to Mort Lowenthal, Frank Brunetta, Linda Phillips, and Ann Miller for their comments and observations, for reading the earlier drafts, and for providing me with helpful, critical insights to substance as well as to clarity and organization.

I am especially indebted to Joan Perry, who gave invaluable assistance in the preliminary secondary research and also contributed to the organization of the book.

LEONARD VIGNOLA, JR.

Contents

ONE

Divestment Trends

"THE HOTTEST AREA in the merger and acquisition game today is the corporate sell-off," according to an article in *Mergers and Acquisitions, The Journal of Corporate Venture.* That comment was made not in 1972 but in 1968. Even then, four years earlier, the present onset of the corporate sell-off already was evident to those close to the merger-acquisition scene. But despite that long awareness of the importance of divesting, factual support of divesting frequency and the internal formalization of the divestment process are still negligible.

In this chapter we will examine divestment frequency and characteristics to the extent that the quantitative data permit. The chapter is divided into three parts: statistical data, results of a questionnaire on internal company organization, and a discussion of the underlying influences that will determine the frequency and characteristics of divesting in the future.

Statistics on Divestment

Mergers and Acquisitions began detailed reporting of individual divestments in its spring 1971 issue, and data are supplied by five issues to summer 1972. Prior to its comprehensive and detailed listing of all divestments, the journal

Table 1. Divestment frequency, 1971–1972.

NO. FIRST QUARTER 1972	NO. SECOND QUARTER 1971	PERCENT INCREASE
157	92	70

kept an incomplete list of individual divestments. Both sets of data have been used to sense the trend of divestment frequency and characteristics. Information on mergers and acquisitions was also obtained from the Federal Trade Commission, but the data on divestments are not segregated.

A comparision (Table 1) of the more complete, recent data reveals a 70 percent increase in divestment frequency between the spring reports of 1971 and 1972. Information on the divestments included the kinds of activities divested and the forms of payment used in the divestment purchases. The divestments were classified as division or subsidiary, product line, investment interest, and miscellaneous (Table 2). Divestment of entire divisions or subsidiaries was the most typical action, but a not inconsequential number of product line, investment interest, and miscellaneous divestments also took place in 1971 and 1972.

An attempt to break down the method of payment used most frequently was less successful, largely because the

Table 2. Divestment category (percent).

CATEGORY	FIRST QUARTER 1972	SECOND QUARTER 1971
Division or subsidiary	64	82
Product line	14	8
Investment interest	12	2
Miscellaneous	10	8

Table 3. Form of divestment payment
(percent).

FORM	FIRST QUARTER 1972	SECOND QUARTER 1971
Cash	60	40
Cash and other	27	37
Noncash	13	23

payment form was not disclosed in over one-third of the announcements of divestment. In the remaining divestments, cash or a combination of cash and some financial instrument was the most frequent payment form. The pattern is presented in Table 3.

There is minor note—minor because the background information is still far from being developed. Noncorporate or private purchasers of divested units increased from 16 percent of all completed divestments during the first quarter of 1971 to 18 percent during the first quarter of 1972. Noncorporate buyers include individuals, employees, and private investment groups. Though the data fall short of substantiating a trend, they suggest a change in the corporate marketplace.

Earlier Data

The 1971 and 1972 quarterly data suggest some 400 divestments in 1971 and perhaps 600 in 1972. Earlier data, from the spring 1966 issue of *Mergers and Acquisitions,* for the period from 1955 to 1964 indicate a frequency of divestment considerably below the 400-to-600 level. In the late 1950s, divestment frequency was below 100 per year: it rose to the 150 per year range by the mid-1960s. Thus from 1955 through 1964 the frequency of divestment more than doubled. It nearly tripled between 1964 and 1971, and the 1972

Table 4. Number of divestments,
1955–1964.

YEAR	NUMBER
1955	63
1956	83
1957	70
1958	76
1959	114
1960	101
1961	118
1962	126
1963	152
1964	134

preliminary data suggest another rise by about 50 percent. The annual data for 1955 to 1964 are shown in Table 4.

A number of other sources convey a sense of increasing divestment frequency:

Business Week, in its August 15, 1972 issue, points to divestments rising to 32 percent of all mergers and acquisitions by the second quarter of 1970 from 12 percent and 13 percent in 1968 and 1969, respectively.

Forbes, in its January 15, 1972 issue, states that divestments were 29 percent of all mergers and acquisitions in 1971, an increase of 44 percent over 1970 and an increase of 75 percent over 1969.

The Wall Street Journal, in October 26, 1971, reported that 80 percent of the companies responding to its survey questionnaire indicated that divestment of one or more of their units was under active consideration.

So the frequency of divesting clearly would seem to be on the increase. The data, sparse though they may be, point unmistakably in that direction.

Organizing for Divestment

With divestment frequency on the rise, the next question is whether some internal company organization has evolved in recognition of the growing importance of the divestment alternative in the decision-making process. To get an answer, a survey mailed to over 200 companies (see Appendix) asked if the divestment function was formally identified within the company organization and, if so, who was assigned specific responsibility for it. Neither set of answers was indicative of accomplished organizational change, but there was some evidence of organizational change in the offing.

The Divestment Function

Companies were asked how, if at all, their divestment functions were organized. As answers, they were offered these alternatives:

A specific person has been assigned or a particular department has been established with this function as its sole or at least primary responsibility.

The responsibility for the performance of this divestment function has been given to a single person or department as one of his or its tasks or responsibilities.

The responsibility for the divestment function is diffused throughout the company, with no specific assignments designated, but the function exists within a management procedure, such as regular profit-planning reviews, or within committees established in the company structure, such as the finance committee.

Over three out of four respondents indicated that the exercise of the divestment function was diffused throughout the company. Nebulous responsibility tends to be confirmed by the response to a question about the identity of the individuals or departments involved in divestment.

Responsibility for Divestment

Companies were asked to "provide specific titles and department descriptions concerned with divestment" if such existed. The answers revealed considerable scattering and multiple involvement, but they did suggest that some semblance of organizational pattern is emerging. Four organizational segments were cited most frequently (Table 5). It

Table 5. Assignment of function.

DEPARTMENT	PERCENT OF COMPANIES
Planning group	54
Division management	29
Presidential office	25
Finance department	25

is encouraging that over half the respondents see divesting as pertinent to the formal planning process; for, as will be developed in later chapters, the planning process or activity is exactly where the divestment function belongs.

Underlying Forces

A trend toward increasing divestment activity appears to be clear and well substantiated despite the weakness of the supporting data themselves. Three fundamental influences account for the trend and suggest that it will accelerate: changes in company reporting, emergence of the planning function, and the growing respectability of divesting.

The requirement that public companies report sales and earnings by division or subsidiary will focus public attention on operations that have not fared well in the existing company environment. When coupled with that greater outside interest, pressure from the company's stockholders, who will also be more cognizant of poor performance, should increase the number of divestments.

The inclusion of divesting as part of the planning process will tend to increase the divestment frequency. When each unit or product line receives a close annual inspection for its contribution to the company's current and future performance, the focus will almost automatically be on the segments that no longer seem to fit. Continued presence in the marketplace should reflect a constant positive affirmation of that presence and not a mere acknowledgment that the company is indeed involved. When the annual review becomes more universal, the desirability of divesting certain activities will be evident much more often. The more frequent the thought, the more frequent the action.

Finally, the sheer quantitative facts of divestment tend to affect management thinking. Increasing frequency has transformed divestment from an unacceptable, almost unthinkable action to a more normal response to a business situation. It is difficult to appreciate that factor fully. When management was inhibited by fear of divestment stigmatism, only desperate situations received serious divestment consideration. Now that there is less fear of disapproval, divesting may be chosen as the remedy for situations that are marginal or just do not fit within the corporate plan any longer. Such marginal situations far exceed in number the desperate ones.

TWO

The Normalcy
of Divestment

A COMPANY LIVES by expanding and contracting, by growing and changing, by acquiring and divesting. These are the actions of a healthy, vital company, not a sick, dying company.

The intent of this chapter is to discuss divestment as a regular corporate activity and to establish its normalcy as equal that of producing a product or service, marketing and selling, or planning and acquiring. That is, the effort will be to fit the divesting function into the framework of company activities. To that end, the chapter will deal somewhat philosophically with the concept of normalcy of divestment and why the concept is so essential to a company. The discussion is actually independent of the fact of increasing frequency of divestment and the reasons why the trend is apt to accelerate, although both fact and reasons lend importance to a consideration of normalcy.

Divestment as Part of Business Life

Divestment is a normal process not just in failing or unsuccessful companies but in healthy, growing, profitable, and otherwise vital and successful companies as well. To establish that point, four facets of business life will now be examined for their relation to the normalcy of divestment: life cycle, judgmental decision performance, evolution of goals and objectives, and acquisition fallout.

Life Cycle

Life cycle is the process by which a being, a unit, a thing is initiated, born; is thrust into an environment; will grow; mature; will decline, die, or disappear. The life cycle concept is most frequently applied to new products, but a facility or a whole business can be seen to undergo conception, birth, growth, maturation, decline, and death. The dynamics of the life cycle can change a company's attitude toward any given activity. At one stage in the life cycle an undertaking might appear to be highly desirable and of great advantage; at another stage, the same undertaking might appear to be quite unattractive and disadvantageous. The change in attitude might be due to changes in the activity itself or changes in the industrial environment in which the activity must function. But when the change of attitude, for whatever reason, does occur, eliminating the activity by divestment may be a very normal and useful response.

An example of divestment as a normal response to changing industry and company conditions is the divestment by Air Products and Chemicals Inc. of its Metal Services division.

Air Products and Chemicals sold Metal Services to ESAB Ltd. The company had entered the welding and cutting market with its division a number of years earlier when the market was growing, and it was confident of its capability to succeed. When it divested its subsidiary, the market was no longer growing rapidly and about 50 companies were competing in it. Further, sales of its own unit had plateaued and were insufficient for the unit to be viable.

Judgmental Decision Performance

Judgmental decision performance has to do with the reality that decisions reflect judgments that are sometimes right and sometimes wrong. Becoming involved in a business activity reflects the company's judgment of future benefits from the undertaking. That judgment may be based on the most exhaustive analysis possible or on nothing more than intuition. In either case, the time will come when actual benefits can be measured and the value of the judgment will then be affirmed or denied.

It is not the purpose of this book to examine why judgments are faulty on occasion. Overlooked facts, changes in market demands, and deficiencies in products play a part. But it is one thing to make a bad decision and another thing to live with it. Since not all decisions about business initiation and involvement can possibly be successful, divesting should be a normal response to an error in judgment. And such an error can occur in the biggest of companies in spite of what would seem to be the most thorough research and investigation and the fullest commitment. Du Pont and Corfam are a case in point.

Du Pont invested years of work and millions of dollars in the development and introduction of Corfam to meet a real need that is still largely unmet with existing materials for shoes. Nevertheless, in spite of all of the efforts and precautions, subsequent performance fell far short of minimum expectations. Du Pont finally recognized the failure and divested much of the operation.

Evolution in Goals and Objectives

Attitudes toward goals and objectives obviously can change; what was once important can become inconsequential. There is the story of the young boy who went off to college concerned at how narrow and unknowledgeable his father was. When he returned four years later, he was astonished at how much his father had learned and broadened during the intervening time.

In some instances, the changes can be entirely internal. The most obvious examples are troubled companies whose instinct to survive supersedes other corporate objectives. Divestments in the early 1970s by such well-known companies as LTV Corp. and Boise Cascade reflected a change from a pursuit of growth and expansion in the industries and markets of the divested activities to the single, simple pursuit of survival.

But a company's goals and objectives can change in fundamental ways that are not the result of such compelling pressures as survival. ITT's divestment of several companies in order to acquire an insurance company reflected a shift in corporate objectives, at least in part. A second example is supplied by the steel industry. Immediately after World War II steel companies sought to secure control of their sources of ore and coal. That objective was common to both the largest companies and the intermediate-size ones. Some ten or fifteen years later, however, attitudes toward the importance of company-owned and -controlled raw material sources had changed substantially, especially among the middle-size steel companies.

Crucible Steel had acquired and reactivated some coal mines in West Virginia. But it became clear by the late 1950s and early 1960s that changes in coal-mining operations and steel-making techniques, along with an abundance of coal, would enable Crucible to obtain long-term contracts to meet its coal requirements at a much lower cost than it could achieve by mining its own coal. The decision was to sell its mines.

When industry environmental changes affect goals and objectives, it is quite usual for certain activities to no longer

fit as well as they once did. The normal consequences
of such changes might best be served by divestment.

Acquisition Fallout

Acquisition fallout does not have the philosophic orientation
of life cycle, judgmental decision performance, and evolution of goals and objectives; instead, it finds its rationale
in the nature of mergers and acquisitions. Frequently, an
activity that is included as part of an acquisition is not
actually wanted by the buying company. Sometimes that
is recognized at the time of the acquisition and immediate
steps are taken to separate the activity.

A large foreign financial group expressed interest in acquiring
an American insurance and consumer finance company. However,
the sought-after company also operated a large chain of retail
home furnishings outlets. A condition to the acquisition was
to find another buyer for the chain of retail stores.

On other occasions the activity is just passed along as
part of the total acquisition; then it flounders until the
new management recognizes the non fit and either provides
it with more support and a strengthened base or divests
it.

In 1965 the Pepsi Cola and Frito-Lay companies merged. The
commonality of their distribution systems and retail markets was
most apparent. However, within the Frito-Lay group of companies
was a small operation that manufactured and sold prepackaged
condiments for the institutional food market. Neither the typical
customer for snack foods nor the route truck distribution system
for potato chips and soft drinks related to the distribution and
sale of the condiments. After a number of years of mediocre
performance, the unit was divested.

It should be noted that such divestments are normal responses to situations and are not atypical.

Divestment as a Positive Response

Divestment is a positive response that can be used to accomplish many things. That point about it was established in the discussion of its normalcy as a response to a wide range of circumstances. The reasons why a firm might choose the divestment course of action may vary, but the single purpose of divestment is to sever a firm's involvement in an activity. That purpose, however, is essentially negative in character and no doubt that negativism accounts for the widespread absence of policies and procedures for divesting. It also helps to explain the reluctance of many companies to discuss divestment concretely rather than in abstract or theoretical terms.

Although the cessation of an activity is essentially negative, divestment can become a positive response through its implementation. The reason lies in the psychology of acting in an unfavorable situation versus succumbing passively. Of course, other methods of terminating an involvement do exist, as will be developed in subsequent chapters. The decision to divest must be made after a consideration of alternative courses of action, including increasing and strengthening the company's involvement.

Divesting can free resources that may then be channeled into new opportunities or reinforce existing undertakings. As will be developed in a later chapter, the divesting action should be carried out only in conjunction with a determination of alternative uses for the resources that have been freed.

During the latter part of 1972, Boise Cascade explained its active divestment program as a need for resources, in part, of course, to retire a high debt load.

Divesting can implement fundamental changes in corporate direction or goals. The company's efforts can be redirected through an elimination of activities that no longer fit the company's new goals and objectives and a redeployment of the freed resources.

The ITT divestments made in connection with the acquisition of the Hartford Fire Insurance Company is an example of redirection of effort. ITT's movement toward the insurance market would be abetted by the acquisition. The divesting of certain operations such as Avis Rent a Car System was a necessary and positive response to the government's objections to the acquisition.

Divestment, when it is properly organized and carried out, represents a management process that in itself is positive in nature. That the act of divesting remains largely disorganized in practice emphasizes the negative instead of the positive aspects of the process. Until divestment is viewed as an integral part of decision making, the negative cast of the action will prevent its optimal use.

THREE

The Divestment Situation

A DIVESTMENT does not just happen; it is usually the culmination of months or even years of struggle with an unfavorable situation and the failure of several corrective strategies. An illustration is Crucible Steel's attempted divestment of its West Virginia coal mines.

Crucible Steel's decision in the mid-1960s to sell off or shut down its coal mine properties in West Virginia followed by several years its decision to reduce mining operations because they were uneconomical. Thus shutdown followed several years of curtailed mining. The lack of satisfactory return from the mining operations had long been before Crucible Steel management. Divestment was only one of the several responses to the problem.

Divestment consideration, then, can arise as one of a number of courses of action for meeting a troublesome or unsatisfactory situation. Such a situation can be due to lagging profit performance or losses, inadequate sales growth or declining market share, excessive resource requirements or the need to divert resources to other company activities, government action such as antitrust or expropriation, shift in corporate objectives or strategies, or technological change. The purpose of Chapter 3 is to focus on the point of departure, the point at which divestment is or can be considered. What are the signals that warn or can warn a company that divestment should be considered? What forms of intelligence or information control should be available to assure a company that the necessary signals will be given by the management control system? Those questions will be discussed in connection with the factors in unfavorable situations.

Lagging Profit Performance

A major, if not the major, reason for a company to decide that it wants out of a business is that the activity simply is not making either the kind of return expected of it or the return that could be made by some alternate use of the resources employed in it. Since profit is the central objective of business and the principal motivation for any company undertaking, management is especially alert to the extent and direction of profit. Conceptually, probably no other signal of possible divestment is as easy to understand; in practice, no other signal is as difficult to generate. The questions that arise at once are what profits are adequate, how profits are related to the resources employed, and what profits represent. Because of the importance of the profit signal in potential divestment situations, a hypothetical example is presented in Table 6.

Table 6. Company X.

	DIVISION A	DIVISION B	DIVISION C	CORPORATE TOTAL	
Sales	$200	$100	$50	$00	$350
Cost of sales	120	70	40	00	230
Gross profit	80	30	10	00	120
Overhead	40	15	5	25	85
Pretax profits	40	15	5	(25)	35

Most companies have reporting systems that will provide sales and profit performances by division as well as in total. The data of Table 6 show that, of the three divisions, A is most profitable in relation to both absolute profits and ratio of profits to sales whereas C has the lowest absolute profits and also the smallest ratio of profits to sales. So the next question is whether profits are adequate, and the answer is not immediately apparent from the data.

For the information in Table 6 to serve as a signal to management, a warning system would have to be built into the reporting network. It should relate data such as those reported here to certain agreed-upon standards. Failure of the two to agree would alert management. For example, any operation that generates profits under ten dollars or any division that shows a pretax return below 15 percent of sales might warrant automatic divestment review.

The point is that the signal system required is one that automatically informs management that a situation needs review. It does not provide the interpretation or analysis needed; it merely feeds back to management certain preestablished performance criteria for company activities. As a matter of policy, no company wants to devote attention and energy to operations that generate insufficient profits or too low a profit ratio.

The signal system should serve one other purpose, however. It should call forth from the information base much of the material required for a preliminary analysis of the situation. Are the reported profits consistent with previous data or are they unusual? An answer unusual to the question might suggest possible special circumstances that could be temporary.

Cyclical industries, such as steel and machine tools, show quite low profits and even losses during the declining and bottom periods of a business cycle. A company may decide that it does not want to operate in such industries and markets, but its decision should be based on profits generated over the full cycle and not just on the periods of poorest performance.

It is equally necessary that the information system show the direction of profits. Life cycle of the activity can be quite important. Is the operation on the threshold of taking off, or have sales flattened, perhaps even started to decline? The examples of Du Pont and Corfam and Crucible Steel and the West Virginia coal mines illustrate the life cycle influence.

Du Pont viewed its Corfam program as early-stage life cycle. As a result, its tolerance of unfavorable profit performances persisted longer than it might have otherwise while it sought for the needed breakthrough to capture a substantial market.

Conversely, Crucible Steel viewed its West Virginia coal mines as marginal at best. They required deep pit mining, and neither the quality of the coal or the volume of mining that was sustainable warranted continued operations.

A more difficult demand on the information system arises from the interrelation between the divested activity and the other activities, products, and services of the divesting company. Would a divestment impair the viability of the remaining segments of the company? Would lower sales volumes result in uneconomic production runs of the company's other lines? To what extent are the marketing and distribution systems dependent on the sales volume of the divested operations? Could the reallocation of overhead costs following the divestment adversely and significantly affect the profit margins of the remaining operations?

Crucible Steel has been known within the steel industry as a producer of specialty steels—high-grade alloys, stainless steels, and so. However, much of its total tonnage in the 1960s was in the basic carbon and alloy-steel grades. Considerable thought had been given by Crucible management over the years to closing down or divesting the basic carbon and alloy-steel-making operations. Substantial advances in steel-making technology had been made since the end of World War II, and a major investment in new steel-making facilities would have been required to preserve the marginal profitability of those product lines. Such resources were not readily available and could in any case be better utilized for the specialty-steel lines. Yet the divestment decision was deferred because the divestment of the basic carbon and alloy-steel-making operations was expected to put a sharply higher cost burden on the remaining specialty-steel product lines.

There is another aspect of fixed-cost attribution. For divestment consideration, allocations of costs previously incurred are useful primarily for accounting or tax purposes. The costs are not those that will be incurred if the activity continues, nor are they those that will be eliminated if the activity is divested. But only the continuing costs of operation and the costs that would no longer be incurred after divestment should bear on the divestment decision.

Even the fact that all such fixed costs have not yet been charged against current income does not enter into the evaluation. Turning again to the hypothetical example of Table 6, depreciation and other fixed-cost charges can be seen to affect both the cost of sales and the overhead charges to division C (Table 7). The adjusted figures still

Table 7. Division C of Company X.

	ORIGINAL	ADJUSTED
Sales	50	50
Cost of sales	40	38
Gross profit	10	12
Overhead	5	2
Pretax profits	5	10

do not necessarily substantiate the value of keeping the operation or make a case for divesting it. But they do reveal what return is being obtained from the present employment of resources.

Resource utilization is the final and most critical demand on the information system. However, a company cannot always determine what resources should be charged against the various portions of the business. Numerous allocation formulas are available, but they tend to be guided first by the need to divide the resources among all the operations. A primary influence is the use of historical accounting records, rather than current assessments or resource requirements. Although that approach is reasonable and is no doubt justified in accounting for all resources even partially utilized, the resulting overhead allocations may assign more resources to an activity than are actually required to sustain it.

Most steel operations show a heavy commitment of resources. U.S. Steel found that its Donora, Pennsylvania, facility had become only marginally profitable during the 1950s, especially as foreign steel imports began to penetrate such steel product markets as nails and fencing. Obviously, no new investment in facilities for those products could be justified, but U.S. Steel was able to keep the operation active for several years because no new resource commitment was required and the possible freeing of resources was quite limited.

The preceding example highlights an extremely important fact. That resources, even substantial resources, are committed to an undertaking does not mean that they are available for diversion to some other activity. If the major purpose of divestment is to free resources for redeployment elsewhere, that factor becomes critical. The divestment evaluation, then, must be based on the adjusted profits, the resources that are available for diversion, and the possible benefits from the redeployment of the divertible resources. Thus the analysis is essentially one of ranking opportunities, both existing and future. At this point, the absolute or automatic criteria used in the early warning system are not applicable.

At this point in the analysis, the questions of risk and uncertainty and their relation to the various alternative benefit flows should be introduced. To some extent, the inclusion of risk and uncertainty elements in the analysis will make the continuance of the activity look more attractive. Greater risk and uncertainty tend to be associated with undertakings yet to be assumed. The return being realized from a current activity, even if it appears to be less satisfactory than possible alternatives, has the advantage of higher certainty and a better definition of attendant risk.

The demands on the information system are substantial. Beyond the comparatively easy display of the trend or direction of profits, the information system must provide the sales and cost ramifications of the interrelationship between the divested activity and other company operations, separate the costs arising from overhead allocations and fixed-cost attributions, and distinguish the resources committed to the divested activity only.

Inadequate Sales Growth or Market Share

Sales volume and market share are major corporate objectives. Many firms establish their goals simply by projecting growth rates and shares of the market. A company segment in which growth has stopped or is lagging, possibly in association with loss of market position, can be a candidate for divestment. But although rate of growth and market penetration are more easily measured than the profit aspects previously discussed, a number of factors must be included in the final divestment analysis.

Sales growth could be limited by production capacity. Further growth might require an addition to manufacturing capacity that has not and may not be made. But the decision not to commit more resources to an operation is not the same as one to divest the operation. The following example illustrates the point.

An East Coast company in the secondary lead business had, through an aggressive marketing and sales effort, reached the limit of its plant capacity. Accordingly, consideration was given to increasing plant capacity. The decision was deferred, however, because of the long-run uncertainty surrounding the use of lead additives in gasoline. Such a change in demand for secondary lead would, of course, affect a divestment decision. But at the time, the business was quite profitable and there were other indicators of possible future market strength to offset the use of lead in gasoline. During the period of uncertainty, though, sales growth was affected.

Shortages of raw materials can constrain sales growth. Periods of heavy military preparation and even peak periods in a business cycle often limit a company's ability to increase production to meet possible increased sales. Strikes and various natural catastrophes have a similar impact. The steel industry is an excellent source of examples for most of the constraints on sales.

Nickel, a key ingredient in a large group of stainless-steel products, has been in very short supply at various times over the last two decades. As a consequence, certain groups of stainless-steel products have exhibited a poor growth performance.

The degree of marketing and promotional support also can be critical to the sustained growth of a product. Cutbacks in such support can have an adverse effect on sales. Sometimes the effect is delayed.

A major soft drink company introduced a new soft drink and achieved substantial market penetration in the first year as a result of a very effective—and costly—promotional and advertising campaign. Second-year sales performance was disappointing. An analysis of second-year sales revealed that promotional and advertising support had been withdrawn significantly following the successful introduction, and the result was reduction in sales growth.

The stage of the product's life cycle can be quite relevant to rate of sales growth. New products should grow rapidly if they are to be successful; older, more established products should exhibit greater sales volume stability but not as rapid sales growth. The distinction can be seen in a comparison of the sales curves for two successful snack food products.

A major snack food company had a product line that can be divided into two broad categories: potato chips and corn chips. The corn chips are newer on the market and demonstrate a substantially faster rate of sales growth than the older potato chip line. But the older chip line continues to generate the major share of the business and remains satisfactorily profitable, especially in terms of total profits generated.

Finally, sales data by themselves are not an adequate basis for assessing the soundness of a product line or operation. Sales volume, even with very rapid sales growth, is not satisfactory unless it is acceptably profitable. A case in point was a major leasing company that conducted a large and growing business in car and truck leasing.

The leasing company, a subsidiary of a major company, had grown into one of the largest companies of its kind in the world. A large portion of its total business was its car and

truck leasing. It had millions of dollars in vehicles out on lease
each year, and the amount was growing. However, an analysis
of the leasing operations revealed that, although it accounted
for the largest share of the total funds committed, the car and
truck leasing segment of the business represented only a nominal
share of the profits generated—in fact, a very low return on
the resources deployed. The company subsequently divested that
segment of its leasing operations.

The key factors are sales volume, sales growth rate, and
market share, and for all those factors automatic warning
standards can be created. Data on the key factors usually
are the most available information within a company, but
the demands on the information system extend beyond
providing those data. Also required is information on
production capacity, conditions affecting key supplies and
suppliers, and status or changes in status of advertising
and promotional efforts. And no data on sales are complete
until profit information is included.

Technological Change

Technological change can so alter a company's position
that part of the company's operations are no longer competitive; it can cause lower profit margins and declines in
sales and market share. Awareness of technological change
is important because it can provide advance notice of
pending problems prior to any noticeable changes in profits
or sales.

The technological change factor needs to be considered
in conjunction with the many financial factors. Changing
technology by itself, though an independent force, looms
as a possible cause for divestment because of the financial
implications and seldom because of the technological ones.
Put simply, a company usually possesses or can gain access
to sufficient technical or research expertise to preserve

a competitive posture within its market and industry. However, the resources necessary to exploit the existing or possible technology may not be available. Alternatively, such resources may be available but their investment not be warranted by the projected benefits.

The withdrawal of RCA and General Electric from the computer hardware market reflected their respective concerns, in part at least, with the need to upgrade their computer technologies continuously. Clearly, both firms possessed the technical ability necessary to meet the demands. Further, both firms had the financial resources to support the technical effort. Their withdrawals represented their judgments that the financial resources might better be applied elsewhere.

That is not to say that technological change in and of itself cannot have long-term effects. Automotive technology outmoded most of the horse-based industries. Airplane technology made portions of the railroad business obsolete. Technological change was partly responsible for the dilemma that confronted Crucible Steel in regard to its carbon and alloy-steel-making operations.

What kind of early warning and information systems can meet needs created by changing technology? The financial systems reflect adverse technological change too late. A special information system is necessary, and it can be developed from data from the company's own market, sales, field, and research personnel. Those people often acquire information on current and future technological developments, and a regular and systematic process for collecting and evaluating the information that is collected is essential.

Other means of technological information control include perusal of technical journals, listing of relevant research grants and awards, tabulation of pertinent papers presented at the many technical and professional conventions and conferences, reports on product modifications and new product introductions gleaned from the various trade shows and exhibits, and assessments by sales and field personnel of any and all technological information that they acquire.

The obstacle to success of a technological information system is the difficulty of interpreting the voluminous information that pours through the system. Much of what is discussed as possible or future technological advance never materializes. The art lies in differentiating between the bits of technical data that should provoke a response and those that require nothing more than filing.

Resource Requirements

Being in business frequently resembles being in a poker game; to stay in, the company must be willing and able to ante up. Inability or unwillingness is a key reason for wanting out. Divestment, of course, is a way out.

The early warning system for excessive resource requirements rests on a planning effort that includes projections of resource and financing demands. The warning system should provide ample time to appraise the resource demand in light of the expected return.

A West Coast company had three principal lines of business including a division that produced a CRT device. The CRT product line was most competitive technologically; sales volume exceeded $1 million with a backlog of almost $2 million and was profitable. The other two divisions of the business also were profitable and had even better future prospects. The company did not possess sufficient resources to support all three divisions adequately. It chose to divest the CRT division to reduce its resource needs as well as obtain some additional financial resources for its remaining two divisions.

The need for resources can take many forms. When technology is changing rapidly, a company must be able to invest in the necessary research and development programs and be able to finance the resulting new product introductions, product design changes, and improved production capabilities.

It has already been noted that the computer hardware industry is an excellent example of substantial demands for resources. IBM has established the game and set the rules. The companies that want to compete in the market must devise a strategy against the IBM product line configuration and, importantly, commit the necessary resources to counter IBM. The divestments by both RCA and General Electric were an acknowledgment of unwillingness to devote the required resources.

Resource requirements can also include promotion and advertising; for the company must be able to support those efforts at a competitive level.

The earlier description of the second-year failure of a successfully introduced new soft drink product turned out to be an insufficient second-year resource commitment.

A postscript should be added here. Various studies of the causes of business failure reveal that inadequate financial resources are a prime if not a primary cause. Low profit return or lagging sales growth is often due to unavailability of adequate resources rather than failure of the product or service offered or erroneous judgment about the market for the product.

Government Action

The decision to divest is not always internally generated. Government, both domestic and foreign, can force a divestment when none has been contemplated by the company and probably is not wanted. Government action can be simple and straightforward. It may be directed formally and unambiguously at a specific subsidiary or a particular undertaking of a company.

A company's response to government-initiated divestment also can be straightforward, if not overly simple. The company need not develop its own standards; the government has established the standards and now imposes them on a specific company undertaking. Furthermore, the company need not worry about any early warning; the government provides the essential information signals through its official charge.

The government forced Proctor & Gamble Co. to divest the Clorox Co. Its judgment was based on its own standards of restraint on competition and even its own definition of the relevant market.

The preceding discussion is perhaps an oversimplification of possible company positions. For instance, the company could choose to resist the government's divestment action. That course would require the company to develop its own proper legal standard or grounds on which to counter the government's stand. Or if the company's standard were not too different from that put forth by the government as applied to its own operation, the company at least would have its own compilation and interpretation of the relevant data. But the government factor does not consist solely of actions carried out by the government. The company may anticipate government action.

A housewares firm had acquired a major importer to provide part of its domestic product line sales. Although the imported product line was acquired largely to complement the existing, American-produced product line, there was a degree of overlap. The company became concerned about impending government attention and initiated steps to divest itself of at least part of the operation; at the time, no government antitrust action had been taken. The company had established on its own the

legal conditions on which the government might intervene, and
it took the initiative to avoid government interference.

Such concern by a company might be based on informal
talks with the Justice Department or perhaps be a reaction
to a Department investigation of some other company.

Another type of antitrust situation is a divestment required
in return for the government's acquiescence to one or more
of a company's other undertakings. At times, the set of
conditions arises in connection with a company's request
for advance approval of a contemplated acquisition. The
ITT case is an example.

ITT had indicated its plans to acquire the Hartford Fire Insurance
Company. The acquisition would give ITT a substantial position
in the casualty segment of the insurance field. The Justice
Department demurred. After a series of legal battles in the
lower federal courts, ITT and the Justice Department agreed
to an arrangement whereby ITT would be permitted to complete
its proposed purchase of the insurance company in return for
an agreement to divest a number of its existing operations,
including Avis and Automatic Canteen.

Expropriation and nationalization are other forms of
divestment forced by government action, usually that of
foreign governments on U.S. companies operating abroad.
Although circumstances differ from Justice Department
forced divestment, the company in its decision making is
usually confronted with the same absence of choice.

The copper companies have sold their mining interests in Chile
to the Chilean government. Once the Chilean government had
initiated action, the copper companies were left with no choice
but to divest. Much had been done to avoid the Chilean
government's action, and some things about the setting of terms
remain to be accomplished. But the decision to divest had been
made irrevocably.

In spite of the somewhat arbitrary circumstances that surround government-forced divestments, an early warning system and supplementary information backup are both necessary and possible. The early warning system depends on government communication, inquiry, and investigation and a constant monitoring of such government actions directed toward other companies.

The information demands center on the importance of the divested unit to the company, and so profit performance, sales growth, and market share are needed background data. A company is likely to divest an activity that it already knows is marginal in anticipation of government intervention or to concur in the government action without a costly and time-consuming legal defense. And clearly, the divestment of an activity in exchange for Justice Department approval of an acquisition requires a full analysis of the divested undertaking along with a sound evaluation of the many factors involved in the new acquisition.

Divestment Intelligence

The foundation of early warning and information systems is divestment intelligence. And although the various bits and pieces of information necessary have been discussed in connection with specific situations, a general discussion of intelligence is necessary.

A company that finds one of its activities to be performing unfavorably will, at some point, begin to think about divorcing itself from that activity. The converse is that unawareness of unsatisfactory performance not only will negate divestment consideration but also will fail to induce any action directed toward correcting the deficiency.

Therefore, the intelligence system is essential to the entire corporate divestment process. Such a system, however, is not separate from the company's regular information control system; instead, it is or should be an integral part of that system. The reason should be obvious, but a brief deliberation can reinforce the perception.

A knowledge-gathering system that meets the necessary broad and comprehensive requirements is both difficult and expensive to establish and maintain. To duplicate it, even in part, would be needlessly costly if it were not operationally impossible. More critically, the duplicative attempt would most likely result in serious information gaps. Even without an attempt at duplication, serious omissions are the greatest deficiency to be overcome.

Necessary intelligence cannot be defined. Information that could be critical as either early warning or essential backup could appear to be quite innocuous and not particularly related to the operation in question.

A rapid increase in sales personnel turnover can result from a multitude of conditions and not necessarily or even evidently be an indication of need for divestment decision making. Yet the sales personnel turnover could be caused by a deterioration of the company's market position due to an obsolescent product or inadequate marketing and distribution. The company's sales people may not feel that they can sustain themselves, given the company's weakened competitive posture. Of course, such a situation could be temporary and be susceptible to well-defined remedial action. Divestment need not occur. On the other hand, a sales force turnover might point to a more fundamental technological shift that is not so easily or rapidly dealt with Moreover, the technological disadvantage might be such that divestment could be the preferable solution.

To repeat, the intelligence necessary for divestment analysis is generally the same intelligence that is necessary for consideration of the many other responses to unfavorable situations. Thus the response to excessive sales force turnover could be a program for strengthening sales support and training, not divestment, yet the basic intelligence would be the same. A dual or separate control system for divestment, though possible to establish, would increase the likelihood that mundane but essential information would be omitted. And there are problems enough confronting the intelligence system. Sufficient information that can be related to the relevant operations is frequently difficult to assemble, and the problem of measuring marginal or incremental effects is not easy to resolve.

Given the computer base of most middle or large contemporary corporate information systems, the precise form or even substance of reports is not too important as long as the information input to the computer is varied and comprehensive. If it is, the burden really lies with management to ask for the specific information needed to illuminate a problem. Even a number of alternative uses of resources can be fed to the computer for later inclusion in analyses of freed and redeployable resources.

The principle underlying divestment intelligence is that any event, incident, or occurrence bearing on the company, be it direct or indirect, should be noted by company management. Much if not most such intelligence is no doubt insignificant, repetitious, or both. Yet a company's ability to develop adequate responses to the forces and pressures on it demands a system of information gathering that will keep it abreast of all events and developments.

In many ways, the company intelligence-gathering process can be compared to the government one. Various bits and pieces of information are continuously put into the system.

- Sales growth sagged more than usual in the third quarter.
- ABC Company has hired a new research director.
- XYZ Company has changed advertising agencies.

- JKL Company has let a contract for a major new facility.
- The government has initiated action in a new antitrust area.
- Imports from Japan are rising.

The list could be extended indefinitely. Each industry or market, each firm within that industry or market, must establish its own critical intelligence parameters and the trigger or action points for the parameters. A company's intelligence system should incorporate early warning of such problem areas as profits, sales, resource needs, technology, and government action. The signals cannot be expected to be more than initial alerts, but the information system must support the special analytical efforts necessary to get at causes, underlying reasons, and special conditions.

The thought is father to the action. What is discussed in the remainder of this book can take place only if there is an initial awareness of a problem or situation that calls for corrective response, including the possible alternative of divestment. A separate information and intelligence system is not required, but the system that does function within a company must be sufficiently comprehensive to serve in that very vital capacity.

FOUR

Alternatives
to Divestment

THE WORD "OVERKILL" has come into common use to denote
overreaction to a provocation, whether military, social, or
familial. Overkill is found in the business world, too. Take
as an example the competitor who reduces prices by 3
percent and is countered by a 20 percent cut. More generally,
concern over air and water polution has evoked a wide
range of reactions, some of which amount to closing down
complete industries.

As for the subject of this book, a danger in considering
divestment is overkill. It is important to place divestment
in the context of management planning and decision making.
As was shown in the preceding chapter, divestment is a
response to a company problem or situation. But it is not
the only response or even the best or most preferable one.
Moreover, a completed divestment will always be the
ultimate response. Because of its finality, divestment can
be an overkill response to the problem.

Divestment in Perspective

The purpose of this chapter is to discuss divestment as
the final act in a series of feasible company responses

to a difficult problem. The approach will be to look beyond the problem to its cause. Once the true underlying cause is uncovered, attention can be directed to identifying other courses of actions as possible responses before divestment is decided on.

The alternative strategies will be touched upon only briefly. No attempt will be made to discuss cost reduction programs, new product introductions, research and development, strengthened promotion and distribution, and so on. Those alternative strategies are the proper subjects of other books. In this chapter, the strategic alternatives to divestment will be discussed as just that.

Defining the Root Problem

The first step in establishing a company response to an unfavorable situation is to determine exactly what the true root of the problem is. The problem and its root are connected, but they are not the same thing. The difference needs clarification. The problem is the proximate reason for divestment. In the preceding chapter, several possible problems were noted and described: low profits or losses, lagging sales or loss of market share, government intervention, either U.S. or foreign, insufficient resources, shift in corporate goals and objectives, technological change. The roots of those problems are the whys, the causes. The distinction can be illuminated by use of some of the examples cited in the preceding chapter. Take the lagging sales problem first.

A company in the secondary lead business showed lagging sales growth; in fact, sales growth had slowed considerably throughout the industry. Such a situation could point to divestment. But before the judgment was made, an understanding of the basic forces at work in the secondary lead market, particularly the future of lead additives in gasoline, was needed. Possible changes in the legal status of the additives was a known obstacle on the horizon that was deterring further plant capacity expansion and thereby curbing further sales growth. Until the company had an answer to that legal question no course of action such as divestment was warranted. That was the root of the problem.

As another example take RCA's position in the computer hardware industry.

RCA's unwillingness to commit the necessary added resources made its continued participation in the computer hardware market impossible. But the lack of available resources clearly was not RCA's root problem. That it no longer wished to commit the resources needed by its computer hardware undertaking reflected its assessment of its present and future presence in the market. That assessment derived from such factors as product line configuration, distribution and service capability, research and development strength, and technical competitiveness. Within those elements lay the root of the problem.

Other examples could be cited, but the point is clear. A company must seek to understand the causes of the unfavorable situation before it can determine an optimum response or sequence of responses.

Why an activity's performance is below an acceptable minimum is not always easy to determine. That is particularly true when inadequate management is at fault. But many situations with multiple roots require complex analysis. One way to understand a difficult situation is to reexamine the assumptions and conditions that underlie the company's involvement. An example is an undertaking in the manufacture and distribution of cyclamates.

During the middle 1960s a major soft drink company undertook to produce cyclamates for its own use and to sell to the market. The reasons for its entry at that time were most evident:

consumption was then 16 to 18 million pounds per year and was projected to be as high as 30 million pounds within the next several years; the limiting factor was industry production capacity, which was already strained; the prevailing price per pound was over $1.50, which left a substantial margin for profit; and new technology that purportedly allowed for a purer product at a lower cost was available.

Several years later, after it had launched an undertaking based upon the new technology, the company realized it was incurring large losses. A review and analysis revealed the root causes.

Product demand had not increased as rapidly as had been anticipated; the use of cyclamates for food products other than soft drinks was increasing much more slowly than had been forecast. On the other hand, industry productive capacity had been expanded to nearly 30 million pounds, and substantial excess capacity now existed. The combination of slower increase in market demand and significantly greater industry production capacity had created a downward pressure on cyclamate prices, forcing them below 50 cents per pound and thus eliminating any profit margin from all but the most efficient production facilities. Added to those industry problems, the new facility, based on the advanced technology, was not operating as planned: costs were considerably higher than expected and the defective product percent became a serious consideration.

In the preceding example, the problem was the incurring of substantial operating losses. An examination of the situation revealed multiple causes: slowing down of the increases in consumer demand for cyclamates, industry overcapacity, and faulty new technology. Only after such root causes as those are defined, understood, and assessed should divestment be viewed as a possible solution. With that point clearly in mind, it is time to examine some of the alternative responses available.

Alternatives to Divestment

A number of alternatives to divestment are possible answers to problem situations or operations. Among them are (1) continuing as is, (2) shutting down, (3) exploiting an operation, (4) adding products or product lines, (5) reducing costs, (6) reviewing prices, (7) introducing new products, and (8) acquisition and merger. Each of those alternatives can prove useful as a response to a certain situation or problem; each can be preferable to divestment.

Before discussing the alternatives individually, it is useful to estimate their importance by the frequency with which they are utilized in practice. Table 8 summarizes question-

Table 8. Frequency of use of divestment alternatives.

ALTERNATIVE	PERCENT YES
Shut down	89
Continuing as is	63
Exploit the operation	37
Add to product line	61
Reduce costs	53
Review prices	37
Strengthen manufac- turing or distribu- tion	32
Acquisition or merger	37

naire answers to this question: What other alternatives are or have been considered when divestment has been a possibility? It is interesting to note that either shutting down or continuing as is was selected most frequently, although neither could be said to reflect a very imaginative or constructive solution to a problem. That point will become clearer as the other options are explored next.

Shutting Down

Responses to an unfavorable situation can probably be grouped into four principal categories: do something, do nothing, get rid of it, and quit. Quitting is probably the least attractive of the responses conceptually. To do something is at least psychologically reassuring; it is in the great American management tradition of action. Even doing nothing is, in a sense, a reaffirmation of previous positive action decisions. And to sell, albeit at a loss, offers the promise of some recovery and thus represents a positive action. But to shut down, to quit, would seem to be the most bleak admission of failure.

Yet shutting down was by far the most widely explored alternative to divestment. That would suggest that the respondents viewed the point at which divestment consideration became a reality as beyond the point at which viable alternatives existed. Most often for them, in all probability, possible divestment had been sought but unsuccessfully. At some point, each company had decided that it must confront the impossibility and costliness of a difficult situation. At that time shutting down no longer appealed to the companies involved as a negative and least attractive alternative.

The chronology of Crucible Steel's coal-mining operations in West Virginia was described in an earlier chapter. Crucible shut down the mining operations only after it became apparent that the mines could not be operated economically. Divestment, at least at that time, was not possible.

Continuing as Is

Doing nothing, continuing as is, would not appear to be a viable solution to a problem. Nevertheless, "doing nothing" turns up as one of the most prevalent responses to alternatives to divestment. It is occasionally an explicit management decision, but more often it is disguised as "deferring action until . . ." or exists under the guise of supposedly taking some other action. Obviously, it is frequently the easiest alternative to take; pure inertia can carry the company forward.

But doing nothing should not be dismissed as an ineffective management response. Under certain conditions reaffirmation of the company's objectives and approach might indeed be the best possible response. Cyclical or recession-caused problems might well be instances in which nothing more significant than redirection or recommitment of effort coupled with a conservation of necessary resources is in order.

A similar continue-as-is situation is a new product introduction. Losses are most likely during the early stages of the life cycle. At some point, obviously, the company must view unfavorable profit performance as no longer start-up-caused but indigenous to the product or activity. Du Pont's Corfam is a case in point. But until then, to continue on the course chosen would seem to be in order.

Some unfavorable situations, then, may best be handled by doing nothing, continuing as is. To accompany that somewhat negative response, however, there should be an ongoing assessment of the assumptions that underlie the operation and a constant review of their validity.

Exploiting the Operation

A rarely admitted response to an unfavorable situation is to exploit the activity for whatever it might yield while operating and then dispose of it in any way possible. Frequently, that approach leads to shutdown.

Since that alternative inevitably weakens its position, why should a company choose it? There are several possible reasons. The company may judge that it has no future in the activity. Whether external factors or the company's own limited capabilities support the assessment is unimportant. The central point is that the company does not view its exploitation as diminishing the future prospects for the activity—it cannot discern any future prospects. Also, the company may have found no outlet for divestment at any appreciable value. Given that unfavorable set of circumstances, the company should find it most advantageous to recover as much as possible before the inevitable demise.

An example of the exploitation response occurred in the steel industry during the late 1950s. At that time, the industry was beginning to experience the first warnings of major, fundamental problems.

U.S. Steel's American Steel and Wire division had a large integrated facility at Donora, Pennsylvania. By the late 1950s, the inpact of foreign imports of many finished wire products such as barbed wire and fencing was cutting into the U.S. sales of those products made at the Donora plant. The steel-making and finishing capability at Donora was quite old, the possibility of divestment was quite remote. Though no explicit statement of exploitation was issued, reinvestment at Donora was sharply curtailed, maintenance was held to a minimum, and other supportive expenditures were curtailed or eliminated. The plant kept operating in that way until it was closed down in the 1960s.

Even if a company is only breaking even on a full-cost basis, it can recover some of its investment through a realization of sales income.

Adding Products

Continuing as is, exploiting the situation, and shutting down are essentially noncorrective responses; that is, nothing about the response is intended to help to improve the situation. But not every unfavorable situation must be withdrawn from in that way. One positive response is to add to the product line. That is an attractive alternative when substantial economies are possible.

A publisher of specialized materials found that its entry into the general paperback market involved prohibitive production, inventory, and storage costs for its few properties. However, by developing certain items as premiums under special contract to advertisers, the company was able to absorb much of its relatively fixed cost for producing its paperbacks.

Economies in distribution costs also are possible.

A company had a snack food operation in Canada that had been losing money for a long period of time. An analysis of the operation revealed substantial distribution costs per item attributable to its route truck delivery system. One of the answers was to add new snack food products. Thus, each route stop would realize more sales volume with little, if any, increase in the distribution costs. That would allow the distribution costs to be allocated over a wider range of products and sales volume.

Adding products is a satisfactory response when capacity is available and the marketing and promotional costs of the products added are not excessive.

Reducing Costs

One of the obvious reasons why an activity does not show satisfactory profit performance is that it incurs too much cost to obtain the resulting revenue. Sometimes the answer is a pricing change; other situations lend themselves to economies by adding to sales volume. Cost reduction is a similar response. It is a positive step toward improving the cost-revenue relationship.

The family of cost reduction activities is large: cost-reducing equipment, value engineering, work incentives, product design modifications, manufacturing practice analysis, make-or-buy decisions, and cost control programs. Any company might add several examples that reflect its own opportunities. The common characteristic is that all the approaches aim at correcting or improving the cost part of the cost-revenue relationship. Many companies assign this responsibility to individuals or departments or have cost reduction practices built into their way of doing business.

A defense-oriented manufacturing firm had developed a lottery ticket vending machine. Although the market for such machines was expanding rapidly, the company was considering divesting the product line. In part, the tentative decision reflected unit manufacturing costs, which exceeded possible selling prices or leasing rates. An analysis of the manufacturing costs revealed numerous ways to lower costs, as by redesign and simplification of the casing and changes to the ticket drive mechanism that would eliminate some parts and permit economic substitutions for others.

In an industry with depressed conditions, that is, one in which overall profit return is low and many companies report losses or only marginal profitability, cost reduction may not be a viable alternative to divestment. However, if the profit level in the industry is generally satisfactory and many if not most firms show favorable profit performances, a concerted effort to analyze and correct high-cost functions might well be the best strategy.

A soft drink company was concerned over inadequate profit performance in its company-owned bottling plants. Its review of the situation revealed that its various franchised plants were showing quite adequate profit performances; many of them were two and three times more profitable than the company-owned plants. It chose cost reduction rather than divestment because lower-cost operations did exist.

As a broad proposition, most operations lend themsleves to certain cost economies. The question is whether the economies can be sufficient to have a significant effect.

Reviewing Prices

A second possible option when the price-cost relationship is unsatisfactory is to do something about the price component. The pricing review strategy is not as clear-cut as the cost reduction one. Cost reduction means simply that, but pricing review embodies a host of alternatives: both raising and lowering general prices, review of the price discount structure, selective pricing based on customer differentiation, and various kinds of pricing add-ons. Each pricing alternative has its application.

First of all, the level of prices may be just too low for an adequate margin over costs. The problem could be industrywide if rising costs have not been adequately reflected in price increases.

Antipollution measures introduce a new set of cost factors that may have no offsetting cost benefits and thus will require price increases to preserve the profit margins. For instance, the changes in automobile exhaust systems and the lowering of sulfur content in heating oils increase the costs of producing automobiles and providing fuels for heating. Although some cost offsets can no doubt be found, it is unlikely that cost reductions can prevent deterioration of the profit margins unless they are accompanied by price increases.

But the price level situation does not have to be industrywide; individual companies can find themselves in the dilemma.

A prepackaged food division of a large firm operated at capacity with a substantial backlog, but profit performance was most unsatisfactory. Examination of the division's sales approach disclosed that underselling the competition by across-the-board pricing cuts was the means used to keep the sales volume high. Over the years, the price undercutting had severely jeopardized the division's ability to make money. Overstress on price cutting had diverted the division's attention from product quality, packaging, marketing, and distribution programs that could have assisted selling efforts. Further cost reduction relief promised little help; the division required a renewed selling effort through product and packaging improvement and strengthened marketing and distribution to permit the raising of prices without unduly undermining sales volume.

The raising of prices, then, can be a legitimate and reasonable response. When market demand is high or some degree of monopolistic pricing is possible because demand is relatively inelastic, the raising of prices can be a sound approach. But although rising costs such as industrywide wage adjustments are often cited as the excuse, the willingness of firms to pursue that course of action might well be termed following the path of least resistance.

The converse of too low a price level also can occur. Prices may be simply too high; by restricting sales volume and not permitting sufficient absorption of fixed costs and overhead, they may result in diminished profits. The appropriate pricing response might be to lower the general price level until the sales volume is sufficient to absorb overhead and fixed costs and so permit profit improvement. The mass market syndrome is almost synonymous with that condition.

Henry Ford made the automobile industry profitable by lowering car prices, producing on a mass scale, and extending the ownership of automobiles to a greater number of American families.

The supermarket achieved its market dominance and at least initial profitability by lowering prices in relation to the neighborhood grocery store and moving large quantities of merchandise at the same time.

The emerging mass photographic market reflects significant advances in technology for the amateur photographer but also significant price reductions to bring the cost of the product within the economic reach of most people and thereby vastly extend sales volume.

As a general proposition, the higher the proportion of relatively fixed costs, the more likely it is that general price cutting, which might result in substantial sales volume increases, would have a beneficial impact on overall profit performance.

Apart from the question of general price level is that of price discount structure, which can be critically important to an understanding of the role and adequacy of pricing. Discounts may be applied in many ways: quantity discounts, discounts to factors in the distribution system, discounts for advertising support, and discounts to particular customers. Presumably the discounts either recognize cost savings or acknowledge services performed in the distribution of the company's product line. In either case, a cost-benefit analysis will often reveal distortions in the discount structure that could be questioned and perhaps corrected. When price discounts are not market-dictated as part of a general competitive price action, the discount structure offers possibilities for profit improvement.

The quantity discount is one of the most prevalent forms of price reduction. Conceptually, economies in production, reduction of selling effort, and consolidation of billing and collection activities are considered sufficient justification for discounts. However, long use of the selling device has frequently obscured the relation between benefits and costs in such discounting. Unfortunately, the quantity discount is one of the most common avenues to general price reductions, and so it may represent a reaction to overall market and competitive pressures rather than a real saving in cost.

Another prevalent price discount is that offered to factors in the distribution system. Wholesalers, retailers, brokers, and manufacturing agents are examples of distribution system factors that obtain price discounts. In each instance, a specific service involving the company's goods is concerned. Here there are two points of critical examination. The overall level of the price discount formula, like that of the quantity discount, should be evaluated. Perhaps more importantly, alternative methods of discharging the functions should be examined to support a better appraisal of the benefits claimed. Advertising discounts are an excellent example of this type of discount at work.

Price discounts to particular customers are a most interesting area of price discounting. It is important to determine whether the discount reaches new business—its avowed purpose—or represents a price cut in existing business.

The twofer ticket for Broadway plays is a way of discounting the price to a show for a potential audience that otherwise might not attend and thus provide the production with sufficient support to extend its run. If all or most of the customers are actually new or the discount even eventually leads to new customers, the effort can be worthwhile.

Airfare reductions for students or groups can add to the customer total; if so, they can be beneficial. However, if they only provide price cuts to customers who would have used airline travel anyway, they might be responsible for some of the current unfavorable profit performances in the airline industry.

The question of price discounting, then, is not simply one of how high or how much the discount should be; it is whether introducing or increasing a price discount rather than just lowering or eliminating it might not result in the needed improvement in profit performance.

Research and Development

Research and development can embrace new products or new production techniques. The level and quality of a company's technology, if deficient, can place the company at a decided competitive disadvantage. Contrariwise, of course, a high level can give it a competitive edge.

The inability of commuter or third-tier airlines to achieve profitability reflects to some extent the failure of technology to provide a small, economical, and easily serviced airplane.

But the question before the company that finds itself in an unfavorable technological position is really whether it can or wants to stay in that game. Problems of technology hinge less on technological possibilities or probabilities and more on the financial will and capability to fund the necessary technological effort. The RCA computer hardware example is one such instance.

A company with a machine tool division was confronted with a serious competitive problem when numerical controls were introduced into machine tooling. Should it or could it divert the necessary resources to catch up was the question, and not the problem of the new technology itself.

On the other hand, technological advances have opened substantial new markets. Advances in copying technology have made Xerox almost a generic term, and a mass market for the home photographic industry has been created by technical advances.

Strengthening Manufacture or Distribution

A traditional company response, honored more in rhetoric than in practice, is to do a better job. Actually, however, both the manufacturing and distribution practices of a company can be strengthened by doing nothing more novel than a better job of management. That alternative is not discussed in this book because the specific actions that emanate from it include a host of things that either seem quite obvious or should have been part of the operating practices all along.

Or Merger Acquisition

The final alternative to divestment is to acquire or merge with what is necessary to make the operation a success. The merger-acquisition route could well be a precarious one because the company may only be buying a set of similar difficulties. However, the merger-acquisition alternative does offer some interesting possibilities.

A snack food company had exhausted all available capacity and was constrained by its manufacturing facility from realizing much of its potential growth market. Yet profit return was too low to justify building additional plant, given overall available capacity in the industry. An answer was the acquisition of a local snack food company that provided the company with additional, modern plant capacity. That step resulted in lower costs, increased overall sales, greater overhead absorption, and more economical product distribution into new markets.

Airlines offer an example of the merger response. Instead of
divesting certain air routes as uneconomic, the CAB has permitted
selected mergers of airlines—Delta and Northeast as an example—to achieve economies as consolidated companies.

A company can acquire most of what it may lack, even
management, through acquisition. If approached with care,
the alternative can accelerate the solution of problems that
might otherwise have required substantial time for resolution
through internal responses.

Each of the divestment alternatives—shutting down, cost
reduction, additional product lines, pricing review, merger
or acquisition—allows the possibility of future divestment
if the alternative should prove unsuccessful. Divestment,
as a response, is the ultimate action. The legal reasons
for divestment have not been touched on because the
alternatives involve legal strategies that are difficult to
generalize about.

FIVE

Preparing
for Divestment

THE FOUNDATION of the divestment process, as noted, is a control system that identifies and describes situations, either product- or operations-based, that are or may be unattractive to the company. Next, and equally important, is a careful evaluation of alternative courses of action. As stated in the preceding chapter, divestment may or may not be the optimum resolution, but there is little argument that it is not the ultimate resolution.

Those points from Chapters 3 and 4 are repeated here to emphasize the importance of the preparatory steps. Either an erroneous diagnosis of the problem or a miscalculation of alternative solution benefits can cause a response that might well be worse than the condition that needs correction. But when the preliminary preparatory steps have been taken properly, divestment may be concluded as the preferred solution with confidence. The remainder of this book treats the divestment alternative as the optimum solution.

In this chapter the preliminary preparations for divestment negotiation are discussed. Included are formulation of divestment objectives, determination of the divested activity, viability of the divested unit, nature of interrelationships severed, information requirements in divestment preparation, and organization for divestment. Although, in a sense, real divestment preparation begins with the diagnosis and examination of alternatives, it is only here that direct attention to divestment begins.

Divestment Objectives

To divest is to sell a portion of the company. But the objective of divestment is not the sale; it is to meet the need that brought on the divestment action. Divesting can be undertaken for a wide variety of reasons, and a survey of several hundred companies showed that no single reason was predominant (Table 9). It is, however, important that the company thoroughly understand the reasons behind its decision to divest. That understanding can affect the search for a purchaser, the valuation placed on the divested unit, the information assembled for the divestment negotiation, and even the timing of the actual divestment. The truth of that statement is implied by the diversity of the factors leading to divestment listed in Table 9.

Poor performance was most frequently cited as the cause for divesting, yet it represents only slightly more than one

Table 9. Factors in decision to divest (percent of replies).

FACTOR	FREQUENTLY	OCCASIONALLY	TOTAL
Poor performance	40	20	26
Changes in plans or objectives	30	19	23
Excessive resource needs	14	22	19
Constraints in operations	9	17	15
Source of funds	7	12	10
Antitrust	0	10	7

out of four responses. In that portion of the divestment situations, the divesting company may be restricted in its search for an acquirer.

LTV sought to divest its Wilson Sporting Goods subsidiary, which was showing a sound operating performance. As a result, it found an interested party in PepsiCo. However, PepsiCo considers only well-run companies as possible acquisitions.

Close behind poor performance as a reason for divestment came changes in plans or objectives. Included were the plans and objectives of the divesting company or its unit to be divested. In those actions, the company might possess great latitude in the timing of its divestment.

A company primarily in the route truck distribution of food products decided not to go ahead with its plans to develop its distribution of other food products through normal grocery store channels. But its already established activities in that market were functioning adequately, if perhaps somewhat marginally. Though the company decided to divest, it waited patiently over several years for the right transaction.

Nearly one-third of all divestment decisions are made because of resource needs, either as a source of funds (10 percent) or to meet excessive resource requirements (19 percent). It has already been noted how critical adequate financing is to the success of a business. Whether the company is in deep financial difficulty, as Penn Central is, or, like RCA, just does not want to commit any more resources to an activity, resource needs are a compelling reason to divest.

The point that divesting arises for many different reasons will be made recurrently throughout the book. In Chapter 6, on the discussion of possible divestment purchasers, reasons for divesting will be shown to be a factor in the search for buyers. In Chapter 9 the divestment package valuation will be analyzed in part in terms of the divestment rationale.

Defining the Divested Activity

The determination of what is to be divested is not always as simple as it may appear to be at first glance. Divestment may be more a selective pruning than an axing action. Furthermore, some defining of the divested activity may be necessary if the acquisition opportunity as presented to interested parties is to be attractive. Even when the divestment decision is the result of such government intervention as an antitrust action, what is to be divested may require definition.

ITT's agreement with the Justice Department relative to its acquisition of the Hartford Fire Insurance Company included the divestment of several of ITT's existing operations. But the particular units to be divested were not arbitrary and mandatory designations. The agreement by ITT on what to divest followed intensive consideration of the comparative flows of benefits and extensive negotiation with the government.

Although the ITT example is somewhat complex because of the antitrust aspects, the difficulty of defining—or, more aptly, circumscribing—the divestment exists in more straightforward situations. It can be traced to two basic causes: delineation of the product line for divestment and division of the manufacturing and distribution facilities between the divested and retained units. Both elements require some elaboration.

Product Line Delineation

The nature of the product line delineation difficulty can be summarized in a simple business truism: a company is not comprised of several contiguous but discrete activities; instead, even if it is organized into separate, legally distinct divisions, it is a collection of differentiated but not necessarily isolated undertakings. The RCA case is an excellent example of the product line delineation problem.

RCA had positioned itself as a full-line participant in the computer market—from sophisticated hardware to peripheral equipment to service and service bureaus. Each of those operations related in some degree to each of the others, and yet each was independent and separately and singularly approached its respective marketplace. RCA determined that only the computer hardware segment of the business required divesting.

The RCA case is a rather clear-cut example of a decision being made within a predetermined segment of a business. On occasion, that kind of review can be carried across the broad spectrum of the company's total activity.

Diamond Shamrock sold a portion of its Nopco Chemical Division urethane systems foam business to Stepan Chemical Co. It indicated that the divestment was part of a continuing program to withdraw from businesses that were too far removed from its basic operations or in which it did not occupy a sufficiently significant marketplace position.

Perhaps the need to distinguish the wheat from the chaff occurs in only a minority of all potential divestment possibilities; statistics on the point do not exist. Many of the recent divestments of such multi-industry companies as Beck Industries, Whittaker Corp., and even American Standard Inc. (New York) seem to be well-defined and separate segments of the respective companies. Yet the principle remains that what is to be divested should be examined closely for portions that might better remain with the company.

Production versus Distribution Segments

Frequently a divestment reflects a decision to prune certain portions of a company's operation—to strengthen the operation rather than withdraw from it. Such a divestment affects only part of the company's capability.

In late 1971 Sonesta International Hotels Corporation announced plans to sell its London and Milan hotels. It was not withdrawing from the hotel business; it was simply selling off part of its sales capability to strengthen the financial resources behind its remaining operations.

The following example presents a similar situation, but with a slightly different twist.

When the Newark News agreed to sell its Sunday edition to the *Star Ledger,* its long strike had just ended and its financial strength had been severely impaired by that strike. By selling its Sunday edition, the *News* gained the necessary resources to rebuild its daily edition.

Divestment of a portion of the physical plant also is a common action.

Schlitz found that the potential for expansion at its Brooklyn facility was limited. It had recently opened two new breweries in North Carolina and Tennessee and felt it had sufficient overall capacity. It divested its Brooklyn plant.

Even antitrust action can take the form of the divestment of facilities but not necessarily the business.

The court ordered the divestment of ten of Frito-Lay's snack food plants. As in the Schlitz divestment, Frito-Lay expected to continue to compete aggressively in the markets being served by the plants. It intended to replace the divested capacity with new plants.

As a matter of strategy, deliberation over what portion of the production or distribution facilities to divest parallels discrimination among product lines to be sold. Divestment need not consist of total withdrawal from a market; it can be confined to a selective pruning of facilities, products, or activities that would significantly strengthen the firm's position in that market.

Viability of Divested Unit

The preceding discussion focused on a prospective divestment from the viewpoint of the divesting party, but a company cannot similarly limit its examination of a prospective divestment. In defining the unit to be divested, it must keep in mind the necessity of offering something viable to the potential buyer. Chapter 6 is devoted to a consideration of prospective purchasers, so nothing more about the buyer need be said at this point. Instead, the concept of viability of a divested unit will be expanded.

By definition viability means a sort of self-sufficiency, and that would seem to imply a minimum level of profitability as requisite to continued survival. Such a meaning, however, is not intended for viability as it is used here. Viability is meant to say only that the divested unit is able to contribute something of value, a stream of benefits to the buyer. The contribution must usually be derived from conditions in the new setting that did not exist or were not possible in the old one.

The divested unit may have its capital base restructured by the purchaser. That would not only improve its reported return on capital but also be likely to eliminate some fixed charges.

A seafood company had gone into bankruptcy. In order to discharge certain obligations, it sold several of its losing operations consisting of fishing fleets and processing facilities. High capital and lease costs made a profitable return on those operations impossible for the divesting company. However, at the price that the new owners had to pay for the facilities, the annual costs became absorbable and a reasonable return could be shown.

The divested unit may be able to realize substantial economies in lower overhead costs. Such a realignment may be achieved when a former subsidiary is set free and is no longer subjected to arbitrary allocations of corporate overhead charges.

A large European plate glass producer divested its losing American operations. The management of the division, with the aid of outside financing, took over the company and proceeded to run it as a separate operation. The turnabout into profitable operation was in part due to the elimination of substantial corporate headquarters charges.

The divested unit may find that a number of former constraints on decision making have been removed; no longer must it observe certain prohibitions or be forced to perform certain activities. A critical area in which some improvement might perhaps be achieved is restrictive labor practices.

The Chicago and Northwestern Railroad was divested to its employees. One of the objectives, or fond hopes, was that under those new auspices the management would have a better chance to modify certain restrictive and costly work practices.

Finally, the purchaser may be able to exploit opportunities more effectively because management incentive has been renewed by the change. Part of the increased motivation might be attributable to such changes as a restructured capital base or release from excessive overhead charges, but part may be due simply to a new sense of life derived from the interest affirmed by the acquisition.

Downe Communications, Inc. acquired the subscription fulfillment facilities of Cowles Communications, Inc. to provide data processing services for its own publishing and direct mail operations. Such facilities became less useful to Cowles following its shutdown of *Look* magazine. The management connected with the Cowles operation no doubt felt an uplift by being placed in an environment where the need for the service was high.

Successful divesting means providing a prospective buyer with something valuable to the buyer's business even though what is divested no longer has value to the divesting company. To find, to understand, and to convey a measure of that value is the key step in the preliminary preparations for divestment.

Other Relationships Affected

Preparing for divestment includes resolving the host of problems associated with the divested portion. A divestment more often than not has a direct impact on other segments of the company than the segment being divested. Other markets or customers or other working relationships may even be put into jeopardy by the contemplated divestment. For example, sales of other products or services may be directly or indirectly connected with the segment of the business being sold.

The sale of its Sunday edition by the Newark News, although undertaken to obtain the resources necessary to strengthen the daily issue, might cause a diversion of the Sunday reader that would have an adverse impact on circulation.

What happens to ongoing contracts a division of a company may hold? If they are not handled properly in a divestment, could there be an adverse impact on remaining segments of the business?

RCA had ongoing service and support relationships with its customers for its computer hardware product line. In its divestment to Sperry Rand, it specifically provided for the assumption of those service obligations by Sperry Rand.

In some cases, production facilities are divested, but the company intends to remain in the market. Replacement of the divested production capability may have a long-term solution, but the company needs firm answers to its transition requirements.

PepsiCo's Frito-Lay subsidiary had to divest ten snack food plants, by court order, but was not compelled to withdraw from those markets. Provisions were included in the divestment agreement to assure Frito-Lay a continued supply from those plants during the transitional phase in which it constructed its own facilities.

In a similar case a company sold the office building that housed its headquarters. Although it had new headquarters under construction, it had to include in the divestment agreement a specific provision for its continued use of its quarters in the building. In another instance the divesting company needed to provide for almost indefinite future use of the divested facilities.

Cowles' sale of its subscription fulfillment facilities to Downe included in the agreement a requirement that Downe would perform whatever subscription services that might be required by Cowles in connection with the *Look* magazine subscription list that Cowles retained.

The possible effect on supplier relations also should be kept in mind; remaining supplier agreements with the divesting company could be affected by the divestment.

In its sale of Steak 'n Shake to the Franklin Corp., Longchamps, Inc. had to review its food supply contracts to determine whether any were predicated on the volume generated by Steak 'n Shake orders.

Some of the relationships to be considered may seem quite peripheral yet are in many ways just as essential. Proprietary rights and the use of names or symbols can be involved in a divestment action.

Lum's Inc. sold its 340 fast-food restaurant operations to provide itself with maximum opportunity to expand its activities in the resort field. A holdover problem was the need to change the corporate name, which continued to be associated with the fast-food operations.

To summarize the discussion, peripheral considerations can become quite critical in a divestment. When production facilities have been divested, transitional sources of supply for the divesting company's remaining products or requirements can become important. When products or product lines are to be sold and long-term service contracts have been arranged, the divesting company must determine by whom the service obligations will be assumed. When the divestment could affect the divesting company's supplier relationships, the ramifications must be explored. And such considerations as the use of name or symbol should be recognized as affected by the divestment. The issues raised by those factors must be resolved before the divestment agreement is signed.

Information Requirements

Probably 90 percent of the preparation for and negotiation of a divestment consists of information assimilation and communication. Asking what kind of information must be assembled for the prospective purchaser is like asking a man who keeps a lion for a pet where the lion sleeps. The lion sleeps anywhere he wants, and the buying company ultimately obtains whatever information it wants. Generally included in the information requested are a description of the activity to be divested, several years of financial statements, product catalogs and promotional brochures, inventory data, facility and equipment lists, background on advertising programs, supplier and customer agreements, union contracts, management contracts, and status of any pending or existing legal action.

Each divestment transaction will differ in respect to the specific set of information and data required and, importantly, the timing of the turnover of particular information. For the most part, the information either exists or can be compiled readily.

Rather than dwell on the details of the information requirements, which are essentially very similar to those for acquisitions and mergers, attention is directed to four aspects of requirements that are regarded as particularly important to the conclusion of a successful divestment: future expectations, salient strengths, major weaknesses, and buyer rationale. The conceptual framework for the development of the information and data within each of these categories is fundamental to the gathering and presentation of the materials.

Future Expectations

Basically, the value placed on something reflects the expected stream of future benefits from it. That being so, discussions of financial characteristics such as net worth and even earnings are useful only insofar as they provide insight to what the future benefits may be. Thus it is only in the estimation of the stream of future benefits that reasonable men may differ. And no measurement is more important to the divestment.

For the divesting company, two different estimates are needed. The first is that of benefits foregone as a result of divesting the activity. That estimate should have been made in advance of the decision to divest. Interestingly, such a benefit stream could conceivably be negative: Rather than forego any future benefits, the company may forego future losses.

Crucible Steel's West Virginia coal mines were closed down, but taxes and minimum royalty payments to the former owners were still being incurred. Divestment would have eliminated those costs without foregoing any existing benefits. The imponderable of some future value of coal holdings might be introduced, but its uncertainty would seem to make its impact negligible.

The other stream of future benefits is the one that reflects the expectations of the divested activity for the potential buyer. It is certain that the prospective purchaser is going to project its own stream of future benefits; it is also true that the purchaser's final decision will rest on its own projection rather than on one prepared by the divesting company. But those observations miss the point to be made here. Only the divesting company may be aware of certain existing and potential benefits that could affect both the willingness of prospective purchasers to buy and the value to be placed on the divested activity.

More will be said about desirability and value of a divested activity to the buyer later in this chapter and in the next chapter. As for the divesting company, the better it can identify and project possible future benefits, the more likely it is that a buyer will be sufficiently interested to pursue the divestment negotiation. Moreover, if the divesting company can create an awareness of certain advantages perhaps overlooked by the buyer, it stands a better chance of realizing the higher end of the valuation range.

Salient Strengths

A consideration of salient strengths of the divested activity is essentially an extension of the treatment of future expectations. What the divesting company should focus on are the particular assets, tangible or intangible, that give credence to the stream of future benefits and that might point up certain possible advantages to the buying company. For example, name and market position are important.

Lum's divested not only the 340 fast-food outlets but also the name. The recognition and acceptance of the name can be the essential element in any activity pointed to the consumer market.

Advantages inherent in a proprietary position such as patent rights or long-term contracts should be stressed.

A New England manufacturer seeking to divest its newly developed line of ticket-vending machines stressed the patent features covering the ticket drive mechanism that permitted its machine to handle tickets with less prior manipulation. That feature gave the machines a decided advantage over other machines coming on the market; the patent protection was important to the value of the line.

Of course, the buying company is frequently able to discern salient strengths that are peculiar to its own needs and so are not obvious to the divesting company. The acquisition of either additional plant capacity or a strong management team could be particularly advantageous to the buyer. The point holds however: It is important that the divesting company emphasize the salient strengths of its divested activity to the maximum extent that it can.

Major Weaknesses

The other side of the salient strengths coin is that all activities have weaknesses and deficiencies, and a divested activity would certainly be no exception. Clearly, the prospective purchaser will undertake its own analysis and assessment of the problems and weaknesses of what is to be divested. And the divesting company itself should understand those weaknesses and have worked out a response to queries and negotiating gambits related to them. The divesting company is vulnerable not only in respect to the value of the divested activity but also in respect to its salability.

A soft drink company had built a combination beet and cane sugar refinery. Performance fell far short of plans, and the company looked to divest the facility. It was at a serious disadvantage in its divestment attempt unless it could explain the apparent failure in the technology necessary to process both cane and beet through the same facility.

Another aspect of divestment preparation and negotiation involved is the identification of major weaknesses. To what extent should the divesting company initiate disclosure of such information? A prevalent school of thought has it that secrecy is a cardinal principle in negotiating when the information could be helpful to the other side. The reasoning runs that if disclosures do not prevent the divestment, they can at the very least adversely affect the price put on the divested activity. Most people interviewed in connection with this book indicated serious reservations to a policy of immediate and full disclosure.

The other viewpoint is argued here—that divestment is enhanced by immediate and full disclosure of *major* weaknesses. First, the argument for secrecy rests on the implicit assumption that the prospective purchaser will not discover the weaknesses prior to the conclusion of the agreement. If he does discover them, nondisclosure had gained nothing for the divesting company. In refutation, it has been argued that premature knowledge of certain weaknesses might prevent the development of an interest that, if sufficiently nurtured, would outweigh the weaknesses in importance. But that would seem to leave the divesting company vulnerable in respect to both the timing and the manner in which its weaknesses are established.

Just how real is the possibility that major weaknesses will go undetected? No doubt they have gone undetected on some occasions and buyers have suffered the adverse effects of ignorance following their take-overs. But an approach to divestment based on buyer ignorance would seem to be rather narrow, and so the argument for immediate identification of major weaknesses of the divested activity rests on the positive attributes of disclosure. The disclosure may indeed make the prospective purchaser aware of substantial obstacles to the acquisition. That could terminate interest and no doubt generate a feeling of relief that danger was averted. But should not the divesting company also be relieved? The answer is yes. The time and effort that might have been expended with that prospective buyer could be better used with companies that do not find the weaknesses a barrier to acquisition.

A mini-conglomerate had acquired a small medical company with a blood analyzer line. Partially for reasons of the financial resource needs of the parent, it was decided to divest that company. The success of the blood analyzer had rested on the creation of a strong distribution system to reach the individual doctors' offices where the blood analyzer was to function. Though the necessary plans had been developed, the company had faltered seriously in their execution. The resulting weakness would be prohibitive to a company without its own distribution system. To proceed with a prospective purchaser, no matter how favorable the divesting company could complete the divestment without the necessity of the buyer's actually checking out the distribution requirements.

Equally important to the divesting company is the control it exercises over how the weaknesses are to be shown; it can place them in their optimum setting. Answers, combinations, and possible resolutions can accompany the disclosure and show the problems in the best possible light. In a sense, it is the argument that the best defense is a good offense.

Crucible Steel's coal mines were high-cost operations because of the layout, coal concentration, and coal quality. Those conditions represented major obstacles to serious divestment discussions. A counterthrust was developed by presenting the details of those facts within the context of a long-term contract with Crucible to take a portion of the coal at a favorable price.

Finally, disclosure creates an image of seller openness and frankness and thus encourages the sense of mutual trust that is vital to the successful conclusion of any negotiations. Since information and data communication are the foundation of negotiations, the prospective purchaser could become leery over completing the transaction if it begins to uncover certain conditions that it feels not only should have been disclosed but were seemingly disguised. Unless the divesting company assumes that the prospective purchaser is too obtuse to ferret out the critical weaknesses and deficiencies prior to the close of the divestment agreement, it must assume that the difficulties will be posed by the buyer either as a barrier to acquisition or as an argument for a lower valuation. Either way, the divesting company would have been in a better position if had initiated the discussions of weaknesses on its own terms.

Buyer Rationale

Much of the preceding discussion has to do with providing a rationale for a prospective purchaser. A forecast of future benefits, the outlining of the salient strengths of the divested activity, and the provision of answers to the problems and weaknesses of the activity to be divested are necessary for the establishment of that rationale.

A divestment is a sales transaction. As the seller, the divesting company should attempt to define how a prospective purchaser can benefit from the sale and then direct its selling effort at the anticipated benefit. That is how effective selling is done; that is how a divestment can best be concluded. The information and data should be prepared and presented as in a selling function.

Organization for Divestment

The divesting process remains outside the organizational structure of most companies. The survey of corporate divestment practices touched in two ways on the absence of consensus on organizational handling of divestment. First, on the question of where in the organization divestment would be initiated, nearly 80 percent of the respondents indicated that the action could be initiated anywhere in the company. No assignment of responsibility had been made. Second, on the question of who becomes involved in divestment preparation, a wide scattering of responses was received (Table 10).

The organizational pattern for divestment remains to be set within most companies, but the frequency of divestment today is such that a casual response is no longer defensible.

Table 10. Involvement in divestment.

DEPARTMENT	PERCENT RESPONDING
Planning	31
Division management	19
Vice president	19
Finance department	17
Office of president	14

Certain considerations do, or should, bear on the organizational preparation for and the undertaking of divestment. The divestment decision is too important, and too final, not to involve the president. Although it is not necessary for the involvement to be continuous, the president must be involved in the decision to divest and he must approve the divestment strategy. Also, the specific divestment agreement must be acceptable to him for its presentation to the board of directors.

Next, it is essential that the entire divestment consideration—the discernment of the problem and the identification and evaluation of alternatives—be part and parcel of comprehensive planning effort. Only then can companywide considerations be introduced and assessed before they are brought to the attention of the president. And only then should divestment decisions be made.

Finally, it is important that key personnel associated with the divested activity be included in the divestment consideration. Obviously, it is difficult or even impossible to explore alternatives to divestment without involving the management of the divested activity. That management might be helpful in identifying and assessing prospective purchasers. In addition, it should not be forgotten that many of the details of divestment negotiations may best be handled by the division's management.

SIX

Selecting
Prospective Purchasers

It is not enough for a company to want to sell a portion of itself; someone must want to buy it. And to find prospective purchasers, or even one prospective purchaser, is not a simple task. Many of the reasons why a company thinks it expedient to divest may be applicable to possible buyers also. Further, and equally important, the goal of the divesting company should be to obtain the best possible terms and not just any terms at all.

A study by Ansoff, Brandenburg, Portner, and Radosevich, *Acquisition Behavior of U.S. Manufacturing Firms, 1946 to 1965,* revealed that acquisitions were most successful when careful prior planning was undertaken by the acquiring firm.* Divestments can be thought of as reverse acquisitions, and so the same conclusion would hold. A divestment is accomplished most effectively when it is planned carefully and not undertaken haphazardly. Essential to the planning effort is the selection of the prospective purchaser.

In this chapter prospective purchasers are discussed. They include internal ones such as employees, managers, and former owners and external ones such as competitors, geographically separated but allied firms, suppliers, cus-

*Nashville, Tenn.: Vanderbilt University Press, 1971.

tomers, and product-related companies. Further afield are companies in industries with either comparable manufacturing facilities or similar marketing and distribution systems and conglomerates, investing groups, or individuals just looking for companies to acquire. Each of the prospective purchaser categories is analyzed for reasons of interest and the problems that might be confronted.

Internal Purchasers

The first group of prospective purchasers to be explored are the possible interested parties within or associated with the company. Not only are they most familiar with the activity to be divested and the easiest to contact but, if they are not contacted, they could well jeopardize a successful divestment with another party.

It is not unusual for management of the divested activity to be receptive to the buy-out and even to initiate the inquiry. That interest is most likely to surface when divestment is prompted by the unwillingness or the inability of the divesting company to support the divested activity. Division management may feel that, given control, it would be able to provide the necessary resources and establish a more positive direction. The willingness of the divested activity's management to step in has received affirmation from more than one private investment group that offered to put up much of the financial backing necessary for the take-over.

In early 1972, International Utilities Corp. announced the sale of its Bradford-White Corp. subsidiary to the unit's management. The divestment occurred because the subsidiary did not fit into the long-range plans of the parent. The new owners included the president and executive vice president, who continued to serve in those capacities. They felt the opportunity would be greater when they were no longer hampered by an overseeing company that was not interested in the market.

The inside group may be a logical prospective purchaser, but it is not always a viable one. Frequently it does not possess a pool of funds from which to complete the acquisition. Purchase proposals from such parties often consist of a pay-out procedure that derives funds from the earnings of the divested activity. That method of payment greatly increases the danger that the divesting company will never receive the amounts due it.

Second, the inside buyers group could be troublesome in the negotiation of a divestment agreement because of its familiarity with the situation. Knowing as it does why the company chooses to divest and the exact nature of the various deficiencies, the group could be extremely difficult to deal with. The psychological position of the divesting company and the inside group seeking to acquire one of its activities weighs heavily in favor of the inside group. The company may need the continued efforts of the group to sustain the remaining viability of the enterprise, particularly as it relates to other company activities. Furthermore, the good offices of the activity's management may be essential if the divesting company decides to divest through buyers other than the management.

The other inside group consists of former owners. They could be the management of the activity, or they could be disassociated with the activity but close to the industry or market. Frequently, they are stockholders in the divesting company and thus are aware of the difficulties that have caused divestment to be considered. They may look forward to the chance to restore the vitality of the activity that they feel was lost through absorption by the larger company.

Whittaker Corp. embarked on a broad divestment program aimed at reducing its total outstanding debt and providing additional financial resources to support its remaining operations. Further, it aimed to concentrate its activities in fewer areas such as metals distribution, housing, textiles, chemicals, recreation, and transportation. It selected Ivy Hill Lithograph Division for divestment because its business fell outside of that market. The purchasers were the former founders and owners, who reassumed the old name and indicated that operations would continue under the same management.

At times, sales to former owners are not very amicable. Occasionally that settlement is the culmination of either a long legal battle or a fierce struggle for power within the divesting company.

Universal Container Corp. agreed to sell its Port Electric group of companies back to the original owners. The acquisition had taken place in 1968; in 1971 the former owners and now shareholders of Universal Container led a dissident group in a proxy fight to unseat the management of Universal. Although they were unsuccessful, they did succeed in obtaining three board seats. As part of the divestment agreement, the opposition group agreed to withdraw.

Other problems arise in dealings with former owners. An emotional barrier may be erected if the divesting company feels that the dilemma forcing it to divest resulted, even in part, from failed objectives or some misleading data and information from the former owners. On the other side of the table, the former owners may approach the buy-back with excessive fervor that reflects their own disappointment with what happened to their company following its acquisition by the divesting company. In either case, the negotiating can become quite strained.

Two other obstacles in dealing with insiders for the divestment purchase should be noted. Board approval is required for the transaction. When insiders or key personnel are involved, questions such as conflict of interest and adequate valuation to the divesting company's stockholders become more acute considerations than if the same divestment agreement had been concluded with an outside party.

RT Systems, Inc. agreed to sell its U.S. Van Lines Inc. subsidiary to a group headed by the chairman and the president of RT Systems. The transaction involved primarily an exchange of stock; the purchasers gave up their holdings in the divesting company in return for the divesting company's shares of U.S. Van Lines. Previously, the U.S. Van Lines operating rights had been written down on RT Systems' books, which permitted the divesting company to show a small extraordinary gain as a result of the divestment. Because the purchasing group had been in a position to influence the original write-down as well as affect the divestment agreement, the transaction could be more vulnerable to criticism and legal intervention by unhappy stockholders.

The second of the two obstacles arises from possible repercussions among the divesting company's remaining activities and management personnel. The distinct possibility of pressure from other inside groups for similar divestment agreements must be considered.

These two cautions are introduced not to suggest that inside groups do not represent a useful and in some cases a preferred buyer prospect, but to outline areas of concern. The divestments have the potential of becoming extremely sticky.

Purchasers Within the Industry

Prospective purchasers from within the industry are the most obvious ones, and typically they are the first to be thought of in the search for a buyer. After all, who might be more interested in a particular activity than a company already involved in either it or an allied one? An immediate competitor is a logical purchaser prospect because the acquisition can expand its own sales volume and improve

its competitive position. Furthermore, and quite importantly, who would be more likely to want to buy certain activities
such as a chain of retail gasoline service stations than a
firm already in and familiar with the market? Similarly,
who else but a computer hardware company would really
want to acquire another company's computer hardware line?

The RCA divestment to Sperry Rand bears on this point. RCA
explored a possible divestment among a number of alternative
purchasers. Only from Sperry Rand, with its opportunity to
broaden its customer base, did RCA feel it was able to obtain
a reasonable price in the divestment.

Second, competitors that have not yet penetrated the
geographic market served by the divested activity should
be good prospects. They are familiar with the business
and could benefit substantially from a geographic boost.
In addition to the various domestic regional companies,
foreign companies trying to enter the U.S. market could
be excellent buyer prospects.

Atlantic Richfield attempted to sell a number of former Sinclair
Oil properties in 14 western states to an American Petrofina,
Inc. subsidiary. Possible buyers for a chain of retail gasoline
stations are rather limited in number. Also, many of them would
be constrained by possible antitrust actions. American Petrofina
is a foreign company, and so one that hopefully avoids U.S.
antitrust proceedings, and it is interested in expanding its
penetration into the U.S. market. It is sufficiently familiar with
retail gasoline operations.

Third, companies that handle similar products but nothing
quite comparable with what is being divested are potential
buyers. The divested activity would be expected to fit into
the acquirer's operations and enhance those sales as well
as contribute its total sales volume.

A company sought to divest its home cleaner product division. The division did not fit well into the remaining operations of the firm, nor did the divesting company feel that it was in a position to allocate the resources necessary to exploit the product's potential growth and profitability. One interested party was a company in the home appliance field. The prospect was actively seeking new products with a high growth rate potential to sell in its existing market.

Fourth, suppliers and customers of the divested activity may have an interest; some of them may have long been attracted by the potential benefits of such vertical diversification. The customer may be looking for a captive supplier, and the supplier may be looking for a protected market. Either one is sufficiently familiar with the operation to be a knowledgeable buyer.

Stokely–Van Camp negotiated for the sale of three of its California canneries to a newly formed Pacific Coast cooperative. The growers who were buying the canneries would continue to supply fruits and vegetables to Stokely. Stokely did not feel the return on its resources in those canneries was adequate, and the growers felt that the vertical integration would provide them with satisfactory economic benefits.

Direct competitors, geographic competitors, companies with business activities in common, and suppliers or customers together comprise a substantial pool of potentially interested parties. They are familiar with the advantages and disadvantages of businesses within a common industry or market. Also, they are probably sufficiently knowledgeable of the divested activity to represent serious prospects.

On the other hand, the problems attendant on divestment to a member of that group can be formidable. Direct competitors pose an antitrust threat; obviously, if the divestment were to result in a significant lessening of competition, the antitrust threat would be most serious.

Yet even in divestment acquisitions in which a diminishing of the market competition is unlikely or by which market competition could conceivably be strengthened, the threat of antitrust action is not to be taken lightly.

Maremont Corp. has been under a 1970 court order to divest itself of 153 auto parts jobber stores and 28 warehouse distributors. Each divestment transaction requires FTC approval. Several proposed divestments to companies that were or could reasonably be expected to become competitors were disallowed.

Sales to either customers or suppliers face the antitrust obstacle in addition to other obstacles that might confront those two groups. Sale of a divested activity to a former customer could impair the unit's sales to other customers that might be competitors of the new owner. Similarly, purchase by a former supplier would put the supplier in the position of selling to customers that have become competitors.

The divestment of three canneries to a growers' cooperative by Stokely–Van Camp avoided the competition problem. The cooperative is still dependent primarily on Stokely purchases, and Stokely will not be affected if the growers sell to other canneries.

Although they have sufficient familiarity with the industry, market, and divested activity to be interested, prospective purchasers from within the industry may also be too knowledgeable of the problems and difficulties specific to the situation to want to pursue a possible acquisition. Also, negotiations with them may be as difficult as with inside groups. Even with those disadvantages, however, the pool of prospective purchasers from within the industry offers perhaps the most likely source and should be given primary attention.

Common-interest Purchasers

Companies with similar production or distribution capacity and the excess ability necessary to handle other products through the same facilities are an excellent source of prospective purchasers. They are frequently searching for items that can fit into their existing operations. Many defense-oriented businesses are good examples of open production availability, particularly for technical or engineered products. The following is an example of available capacity.

TV Communication purchased the CATV operations of Continental Telephone. TV Communication possessed ample capacity to serve considerably more homes in its market area and the divestment purchase enabled it to do so.

Companies with comparable distribution systems or marketing approaches can be attracted to situations or product lines that can be handled with their own products. The products can be essentially the same as or vary in minor ways from the buying firm's product lines or they can be completely different. The commonality of similar avenues to the customer is the only basis for the mutuality.

Abbott Laboratories sold its Creative Touch food flavor line to Early California Industries, Inc. Creative Touch consists of green pepper, mushroom, and bacon food flavors. Early California is in the grocery products field. It proposed to market the Creative Touch line right along with its other products.

Last, some prospective purchasers are interested not because of any existing or former allegiance but because they find the situation itself attractive. Conglomerates are examples—and not only ITT, Gulf & Western, and Litton Industries. Numerous local or regional multibusiness companies have vigorous acquisition programs into which a divestment might fit.

Illinois Central Industries, Inc., a holding company, purchased the Signal Stat division of Lehigh Valley Industries Inc. Signal Stat makes truck and automobile lighting equipment. Illinois Central Industries made the acquisition to replace the profits formerly taken from its Abex Wellman division, which it had just sold to Brush Beryllium Co. The Abex Wellman division was a major support operation in the Canadian aerospace industry. The two operations really had no business relationship other than the sales volume and profits contributed to the parent holding company.

Another example of prospective purchasers interested in the divestment transaction as a business opportunity is the large universe of individual investors or investor groups. They are frequently aligned with investment firms that are searching continuously for sound investment situations; an attractively priced divestment could be of interest to them. Although such potential buyers may not be intimately familiar with the activity being divested, they do possess both the financial capability and the immediate acquisition interest to proceed aggressively.

Boise Cascade sold a number of its resort properties in the Boise, Idaho, area to a private group of local investors. The properties were essentially self-contained and geographically united. The purchasers felt that the resort operations could be viable as a separate and independent enterprise and created a new company to manage them.

A large, almost indefinable number of companies have common interests, be they production, distribution, or just financial. The divested activity could therefore attract knowledgeable interest but present problems of consummation nonetheless. A serious problem can occur when only production capabilities are similar. If the buying company is not familiar with the nuances of and techniques for marketing the divested activity's output, it may never be in a position to exploit its production advantage fully. For example, in their diversification attempts many defense-oriented companies succeeded for the most part in solving the engineering and manufacturing problems connected with the private-sector products they acquired but failed for want of ability to bring the product to the market and sell it for a profit.

Several defense-oriented firms have gone into the mass transportation or pollution control business. Certain design and production problems of some magnitude have arisen, but the principal obstacle has been the inability to market the product lines successfully.

A converse problem exists when the purchaser is knowledgeable about the marketing and sale of the divested product line but lacks the experience and ability necessary to produce. Missed shipping schedules, cost of sales out of line with possible selling prices, or inability to meld design and styling requirements with cost-efficient manufacturing practices can prevent the successful implementation of the divestment.

A large soft drink company sought to divest its sugar refinery. The refinery was constructed to utilize a new technology to permit both cane and beet refining. But operating difficulties discouraged most prospective purchasers. Few companies possessed the necessary capability to even begin to deal with the operating problems that would confront them following an acquisition.

A negotiating problem can arise from the inability of the buyer to appreciate a potential value in the divested activity that the divesting company has identified but lacks the ability to exploit. Unless the prospective purchaser is able to detect and to accept the truth of such future benefits or unless the divesting company is prepared to relinquish hope for the realization of payment for the asserted value, an insurmountable obstacle to the conclusion of the divestment agreement may arise.

Another kind of problem can arise if the prospective purchaser is more interested in the immediate financial gain to be realized through maneuvering in the divestment implementation than concerned over the long-range development of the divested activity. The divesting company could become anxious over repercussions from mass layoffs, shutdown of facilities, and so on. Perhaps there was no other way to salvage the activity from complete extinction, but the divesting company must be prepared for adverse public reaction to the steps taken by the new owner. It may even have to accept some adverse effect on its remaining sales and profits.

Divestment to the Stockholder

A final method of divestment that is worth noting, although it is an infrequent means of resolving the divestment situation, consists in distributing the stock of the activity to the stockholders of the divesting company. In effect, the stockholders receive a return of assets from their company in the form of a stock holding in a new company— new, at least, to them as distinct stockholders.

Actually, this form of divestment is a variation of divesting to the employees, because the variation revolves around the use of the stockholders of the divesting company as the financiers of the divestment purchase. The employees continue to direct the operations but as an independent company, and not as a subsidiary of the divesting company.

The purchase is accomplished by separating the ownership of the divesting company and that of the divested activity. The ownership of the latter is then placed directly in the hands of the stockholders of the former, who really owned it all along.

Genge Industries, Inc. distributed all of the common stock of Comarco, Inc. to its own shareholders. It decided to spin off the Comarco shares because the Comarco endeavor was not related to its other activities. Yet the business was viable and had sound management; thus the stockholders could decide individually how they wanted to dispose of the investment.

SEVEN

Contacting
Prospective Purchasers

IT IS NECESSARY to identify prospective purchasers carefully, and it is equally necessary to plan the approach to prospective purchasers carefully. Several expressions are appropriate with respect to the importance of this initial contact. To paraphrase, ". . . it is not enough to build a better mousetrap . . ." or ". . . if the mountain won't come to Mohammed, Mohammed will go to the mountain. . . ."

This chapter deals with the approach. It touches on the nature of the divestment intention announcement and further develops the secrecy-versus-openness argument, the direct contact versus the use of intermediaries for opening the door, and the substance of the first contact. Once again, the success of the divestment process depends heavily on the earlier steps of that process, including diagnosis of the problem, examination of possible corrective actions, and a careful selection of the preferred prospective purchasers.

Announcing the Divestment

Every activity generates some rumors under the most ordinary circumstances and more than the usual number when it is in trouble. But until the decision to divest has been made, it is questionable whether anything is to be gained by announcing that divestment is under consideration. When divestment has been decided upon, however, the announcement matter must be resolved. Two questions arise: Should there be an announcement? If there is one, how should it be made?

Whether the Announcement

Strong arguments can be made against any divestment announcements at all. They are actually an extension of the general dispute over secrecy versus openness, but their thrust centers on a possible adverse impact on the divested activity of an announcement in advance of a divestment agreement. Potential problems concern customers, employees, and even the company's bargaining position.

Customers of the divested activity could become concerned over continued dependability of supply and begin to divert their orders to competitors. That, of course, would aggravate whatever problems were already affecting the divested activity. On the other hand, the customers might find reassurance in an expectation that divestment would strengthen the activity and so make it more dependable.

An announcement of intent to divest would immediately concern employees connected with the activity. Their work performance could be affected adversely by the anticipated uncertainties of the transitional period. On the other hand, they could be encouraged by the announcement. They could hardly be unaware that not all is well, and so the divestment action could promise a fresh start and new opportunities instead of a shutdown.

Once the divestment intention is announced the divesting company is unable to play hard to get in an attempt to raise the price. Having indicated availability, it must now avoid selling too cheap. According to one school of thought, it has compromised its bargaining position, but the truth of the matter depends largely on how the announcement is made. If the announcement depicts a realistic grasp of the situation and an unwillingness to divest at just any price offered, it could strengthen rather than weaken the bargaining position.

Finally, there is the matter of public image. Could an announcement of intention without a firm agreement possibly be viewed as one more example of the uncertainty surrounding the divested activity? Again, much depends on the handling of the announcement. The divesting company can exhibit a grasp of the problem that can reflect favorably on it, particularly when the nature and severity of the problem are rather widely known and only the company response has been in question. Announcing the intent to divest can indeed cause many of the problems cited by those opposed to openness, but the primary difficulty with an attempt at secrecy is that too often the attempt is unsuccessful. Even if secrecy is maintained, it creates a vacuum into which pour half-truths and unfounded rumors that portray the situation as far more desperate than it is.

The decision to announce a divestment intention should reflect the positive objective of candor in creating an image of being on top of the problem and a willingness to deal with it realistically. If the announcement is tinged with secrecy, its benefits will largely be lost. No categorical statement on the point can be made. Each divestment situation should be evaluated for the possible consequences of an announcement in light of the factors in the specific situation. The announcement, in turn, should recognize those nuances.

Announcement Content

Each announcement to divest should be tailored to fit the particular situation, but some general principles apply:

1. The decision to divest should be presented as a firm, aggressive, positive step on the part of the divesting company. No doubt should be left as to company control of the situation.

2. The continued viability of the divested activity should be stressed, particularly in regard to continued employment for the present employees and a continuing source of supply for the present customers.

3. The benefits to the divesting company should be stated only to the extent that the problems surrounding the activity being divested find resolution, which will avoid the adverse effects on the performance of the divesting company.

4. Brevity is probably a virtue. In its announcement the divesting company should not limit its opportunities for subsequent maneuvering.

If the company keeps in mind the impossibility of being just a little bit pregnant, it will make sure that its announcement of intention to divest will not be ambiguous to the point of leaving more confusion and misunderstanding following it than preceded it. Furthermore, if it is written effectively, the announcement could conceivably open up access to a wider range of prospective purchasers.

Contacting the Buyer

The divesting company must seek out prospective purchasers. It is unlikely that it can obtain optimum value and terms if it relies only on buyers that initiate contact with it. The search divides into reaching possible inside buyers and potential outside ones.

Inside Buyers

Consideration of possible inside buyers, if there is to be any, should be undertaken before outside contacts are made.

Since internal management must be involved in the divestment action, the divesting company improves its chances of maintaining its cooperation by giving its members the preference implied by being the first to be contacted.

Inside contacts are best made directly by officers of the company to the possibly interested individuals or groups, and not through intermediaries. General exploratory conversations should be held with the insiders before lawyers and accountants are brought in so that inside management can feel it was part of the process of developing valuation and terms.

The buyer contact approach with insiders is distinctly different from that with outsiders and may appear to be overly solicitous. However, the good office of the insiders is essential not only to the success of the divestment but also to the current and future performance of the activity.

Outside Buyers

The objective of buyer contact is to reach an optimum number of potential purchasers. The key word here is optimum, not maximum. It is in the divesting company's best interests to contact a range of possible buyers to assure as high a valuation and as favorable terms as possible. However, the appearance of a shopped-around divestment is to be avoided for reasons of maintaining a higher valuation on the divested activity and sustaining the viability of the activity through the transitional period.

Although direct contact is not as critical here as in the case of prospective inside purchasers, companies clearly favor a direct approach over the use of intermediaries (Table 11). Part of the explanation for the high proportion favoring direct contact lies in the intent to contact companies in industries related to the divested activity. Over three-fourths of the respondents to the survey indicated that such contact

Table 11. Method of contacting buyers.

METHOD	PERCENT USING
Direct contact	87
Investment bankers	53
Commercial bankers	42
Brokers	29
Consultants	24
Accountants	18
Lawyers	11
Advertising	8

would have early attention. That suggests personal relationships that could be used to explore the acquisition.

The survey covered mostly larger companies; it was confined almost entirely to *Fortune's* 1,000 largest firms. It is probable that smaller companies might utilize outside assistance more frequently because their range of possible contacts might be smaller. Further, if the staff of the smaller company is limited in its ability to handle a divestment negotiation, the divesting company might well retain outside assistance from the inception of the divestment process.

As a general principle, when personal relationships do exist between executives of the divesting company and prospective purchaser companies, initial contacts should be informal. Even when personal relationships are not too close, direct contact may be preferable because it can facilitate the communication of information that is not usually handled as effectively by outside parties.

External assistance should be used when the search for buyers' needs must be extended beyond the range of the divesting company's personal contacts or when an intermediary may have a better entree to a specific buyer prospect. Also, the divesting company may have a particular barrier to any contact with some prospective purchasers. Here a distinction between the identification of prospective purchasers and actual contact should be noted. As to the identification, the divesting company is well advised to seek advice from bankers, accountants, lawyers, and consultants; the identification process should be as comprehensive as possible before any actual contacts are made. When it comes to contacting specific prospects, the process should be limited at a given time to a few firms, perhaps two or three, that have been selected as the best possibilities among those identified. Also, the responsibility for contact should be centered in one department or individual who will establish the amount and kind of information transmitted. The centralization will facilitate coordination of responses and follow-up.

Initial Contact

A divestment is a sale, and first impressions are important. For that reason, the initial contact is critical to subsequent discussions. It should be direct and brief, and it should be geared to the circumstances of the specific buyer. Beyond that individual tailoring, three points must be covered in the first communication: why the prospective purchaser is being contacted, why the divestment, and what next step is necessary.

Why the Purchaser

Primary emphasis in the initial contact should be on the benefits that would accrue to the prospective purchaser through acquisition of the divested activity. It is essential that the divesting company view the activity from the buyer's standpoint if it is to trigger a response of interest. It should be recognized that the prospective purchaser probably does not have such an acquisition in mind. Therefore, the divesting company must interrupt the other company's

current plans and programs and convince it of the desirability
of giving the divestment situation attention priority. That
is not an easy task, and it can be accomplished only if
the divesting company understands the advantages of the
activity to the other company and directs the potential
buyer's attention toward those potential benefits. The following are some of the possible benefits to the buyer.

1. The buyer will be able to round out its own product
line.

A seafood fisher and processor was threatened with bankruptcy
and sought to divest its U.S. distributor of seafood products.
One interested party was a meat distributor that served many
of the same accounts as the seafood distributor. The acquisition
would help round out the line for the meat distributor.

2. The divested activity may have substantial capacity
that the buyer could utilize and thereby reduce its own
capital requirements.

A Canadian group was interested in selling certain snack food
facilities because of aging and retiring management. An American company had been rapidly increasing its sales volume and
had run out of capacity at its existing facility. Its acquisition
of the Canadian operation resolved its pressing facility needs.

3. The divested products would fit easily into the buyer's
present system of distribution and give the buyer more
weight with its complement of distributors.

In the acquisition of the Ecco Connector division of Phaostron
Instrument and Electronics by Coleman Cable & Wire the
acquiring company looked to strengthen product volume at each
distribution point.

4. The acquisition could permit the buyer to enter a new
market that it had been contemplating but lacked the

necessary base to penetrate. That is the most likely reason for most private purchases of divested activities. As a means of entry the acquisition of an ongoing activity is preferable to starting a venture from the beginning.

The list could be extended, but the point is obvious. It is essential to direct the buyer's attention to its particular reason for being interested.

Why the Divestment

Candor is appropriate when the prospective purchaser is told why the divestment is being attempted. There is no necessity to go into elaborate detail, but the basic situation should be defined. That openness will establish the atmosphere of trust necessary to any further discussion. A misleading initial contact could undermine subsequent negotiations even though a real interest might originally have existed.

Also, the disclosure of the central problem could prevent negotiations that would be a waste of time if the problem were a real deterrent to the buyer. Excessive resource requirements are an example. The buyer will develop its own financial requirements and could become disinterested if the additional requirement is critical. That being so, why take up each party's time?

It is quite true that disclosure can discourage some apparently interested buyers. But assuming that the divesting company approaches the prospective purchaser positively and gives attention to benefits that should accrue to the buyer through the acquisition, it is preferable to terminate contacts for cause early rather than later.

Ending the Initial Contact

It is worth repeating that a divestment is a sale. A successful seller knows how to end a sales contact. Similarly, the ending of the initial contact should be the first step in the divestment negotiations. The primary principle in ending the contact is for the divesting company to leave the purchase prospect with a clear understanding of what should happen next if the buying party wants to pursue the acquisition. The prospective purchaser will no doubt look for a next step such as additional information or a preliminary meeting. The divesting company should state what it understands the next step to be before it concludes the initial contact. It may be appropriate to follow up the initial contact with a memorandum restating what that next step is to be.

The second principle is that the divesting company should strive to retain control of contact and discussion progress. A "don't call us, we'll call you" is not much help to it. If some reply or follow-up is required of the potential buyer, a time limit should be set or at least suggested so the divesting company can be free to act. Such control should be exercised at each subsequent step in the negotiating effort.

EIGHT

Divestment Strategy

DISCUSSION in the preceding two chapters centered on developing a list of prospective purchasers for the activity to be divested and then creating an approach to those prospective purchasers. The next two chapters, 8 and 9, concentrate on the negotiation of the divestment. Chapter 10 deals with the technical aspects of the form and method of payment. This chapter focuses on a divestment strategy.

Three aspects of the strategy for divestment negotiation will be elaborated upon: preselection of a preferred buyer, high and low valuation, and tailoring of what is to be divested to reach an agreement. The goal here is to concentrate on the factors considered important to improving the divesting company's chances for completing the divestment under the most favorable terms obtainable.

Selection of the Preferred Purchaser

Simply stated, the preferred purchaser is the one that will actually acquire the divested activity. On occasion the divesting company may not have the luxury of choosing among a group of suitors; in fact, its task may be to avoid withdrawing or shutting down in the absence of even one willing buyer.

Brown & Sharpe Manufacturing Co. withdrew from the business

conducted by its Anocut division when efforts to sell the assets
of the subsidiary failed. Losses had exceeded $2 million over
the preceding three years, so in the absence of a purchaser
the operation was closed.

Most frequently, however, the divesting company does
have a degree of latitude in choosing its divestment partner,
and the choice is not always the straightforward one of
the highest bidder. Valuation is, of course, an important
consideration, but such elements as method of payment,
timing of the divestment, and implementation of the divestment agreement also bear on the choice. The subject of
valuation is treated later in this chapter. Here the other
elements will be discussed.

Method of Payment

Method and form of payment are the subject of the following
chapter, but from the standpoint of selecting the preferred
purchaser, those factors can be as important to the divesting
company as the valuation placed on the divested activity.
Immediate payment without contingencies and in cash are
the characteristics generally preferred. The degree to which
those factors are critical to the divesting company varies
with the situation.

Boise Cascade embarked on a major divestment program to
reduce its debt burden and provide it with financial resources.
Both immediacy and cash were prime requisites in its selection
of purchasers for the various segments being divested.

A major difficulty confronting the divesting company
is that frequently the suitor who will act most promptly
and will agree to the most favorable valuation will be a
younger company, with all or almost all of the purchase
in the form of stock of the acquirer. The divesting company

must assess its flexibility in the use of such securities to meet its own needs.

Timing the Divestment

The divesting company must understand its own timetable for the divestment as it views the prospective purchasers. If immediacy is not a critical consideration, additional time can be used to broaden the search for the optimum buyer by initiating contact with individuals, groups, or companies that would not knowingly respond to a proposal with tight time constraints. Thus the pressures on the divesting company to divest may be so critical as to exclude a number of prospective buyers.

Time can be a sizable obstacle. For instance, existing management personnel might be willing to offer the highest valuation because of their inside view of the potential of the situation. But they may be faced with the time-consuming task of raising the capital.

A conglomerate decided to divest a regional sporting goods manufacturer that did not fit into its remaining operations. A management group from within the company indicated an interest. However, for certain tax reasons, the company had to divest before the end of the calendar year. The inside group was unable to arrange the necessary financing during the available time period.

Legal issues such as antitrust implications can also be most time-consuming in their resolution. ITT was apparently under no particular time pressure concerning any of the activities it agreed to divest in connection with its acquisition of the Hartford Fire Insurance Company, for the time involved in resolving the issues with the Justice Department covered years.

Through its development of a prospective purchaser list,

the divesting company may determine that certain groups, individuals, or companies would be put in a very advantageous position by their acquisition of the divested activity and so might be willing to place a higher valuation upon it. But some such parties might not be acquisition-oriented or at all alert to the potential benefits. The process of preparing—in effect, educating—them to the stage of negotiation for the divestment acquisition may require substantial periods of time.

Divestment Implementation

Earlier divestment was defined as the ultimate act, yet it may not necessarily terminate the effect of the divested activity on the divesting company. A number of postdivestment ramifications should be considered by the divesting company in its choice of a purchaser. The viability of the purchaser is perhaps most critical. Unless the entire transaction is completed for cash payable in full upon the signing of the agreement, the final success of the divestment may depend on that viability.

The divestment may have been accomplished by using stock of the acquiring company. The actual value received is then the amount that is obtained when the securities are converted into cash. Since such transactions ordinarily place some time restrictions on the conversion—and even if they don't the market may—the stability and growth of the purchaser's stock could be far more important than the valuation agreed upon. An example is the forced Penn Central divestment of Southwestern Oil and Refining Co.

Penn Central acquired Southwestern in February 1970 in exchange for preferred stock that was selling at $26 per share at the time of acquisition. A few months later, the railroad went into bankruptcy and the preferred stock declined in price to $3 per share. Southwestern witnessed the $20.3 million valuation placed on the company fall to $2.4 million within a short time. The Southwestern stockholders went to court to force the reversal of the acquisition.

A similar situation can exist when the buyer uses notes. If, for example, the employees of the divested activity make the acquisition, they may sign notes that they intend to redeem with the projected cash flow of the activity. Inability to meet the note obligations could result in the divesting company realizing a significantly lower return or even having to repossess the divested activity.

Unitec Industries was forced to divest Campbell Chain and Cable because it could not meet the note obligations agreed upon in the acquisition of Campbell.

Other postdivestment ramifications could have serious implications. Would the divestment to a particular buyer have an adverse effect on the divesting company's competitive position in relation to the acquiring company?

The court-ordered divestment of ten snack food plants by Frito-Lay compelled Frito-Lay to give serious thought to the prospective purchaser as a future competitor, since Frito-Lay intended to continue active selling in the areas serviced by the plants.

It is possible that the buying company's handling of the divested activity's personnel following its takeover could affect the divesting company's ongoing relations with its remaining employees or even its unions. It is worth noting in this connection that almost none of the companies that responded to the survey expected employees or unions to be involved in the divestment process. Communication to those groups was confined to information imparted after the divestment agreement was concluded. The whole subject of the employee and the divestment action is covered in detail in Chapter 11.

Divestment could also affect the divesting firm's public relations image, particularly in the communities in which the divested activity was located. Plant shutdowns, drastic cutbacks in labor force, and withdrawal from community support activities and programs could be attributed at least partially to the divesting company even after control had been relinquished.

Valuation Parameters

The first step in divestment negotiations is to arrive at high and low valuations for the activity to be divested. The valuation range should indicate to the divesting company and the prospective purchaser whether serious discussions are warranted. Obviously, seller and buyer approach valuation from completely different vantage points.

Divesting Company

The divesting company must be able to view the divestment results as at least as advantageous as continuing as is or shutting down. Although the reasons for deciding to divest have presumably been defined, it is not known that the divestment agreement at hand is preferable to shutting down. Certain advantages that accrue from divestment are also obtainable by shutting down:

1. Operating losses are no longer incurred.
2. Assets can be written off and the resulting tax benefits can be taken.
3. Opportunity cost benefits are made available by the avoidance of additional investment commitments required by the divested activity.

A company should undertake the divestment effort only if it holds promise of realizable benefits beyond those obtainable by closing down. The benefits could include lower costs associated with a divestment or just the better corporate public relations of sustaining the operation through divesting.

The calculation of benefits serves as a base for the divesting company's low end of the valuation range. Essentially, the analysis that develops the expected benefits forms the rationale for the company's divestment decision. That being so, the analysis underscores the fact that in many divestment situations the divesting company could afford to give the activity away and still benefit substantially from the divestment.

The advantages discussed so far relate solely to benefits that the divesting company secures by ending its involvement. But the divesting company must view the contemplated divestment as an opportunity not only to achieve the benefits already noted but also to recover resources previously committed to and now available for other purposes. To recover those resources, the valuation must reflect possible benefits to the buying company from the divested activity's future and not just the dissolution of its past.

Prospective Purchaser

The prospective purchaser develops its benefits from the contribution the divested activity can make to its total effort, which could exceed the benefits directly attributable to the operation itself. The buyer is concerned with the factors in the divesting company's divestment decision only to the extent that they might affect its own projected stream of benefits or be used to bargain more effectively with the divesting company. Some of the factors that bear on the valuation are readily apparent: current book value versus acquisition cost, projected earnings based on the activity as is and additional earnings from business contributed by the new owner, and advantages accruing to the regular operations of the buying company from the divested activity. But from the divesting company's standpoint, the key to a successful divestment is finding a purchaser that can realize benefits over and above those three.

1. The divested activity may provide the buyer with a quick introduction to a market that it could otherwise enter only with time-consuming and costly effort;
2. Access to more efficient manufacturing facilities or added volume and resulting manufacturing economies without any capital investment cost;
3. Added weight and influence in its distribution network due to the sales volume contributed by the divested activity;
4. Strengthening of its market position and market penetration by the joining of the buyer's and divested activity's selling efforts.

Those four factors can affect possible buyers much differently. It follows, then, that the high valuations of the prospective purchasers can also differ quite significantly. The selection of the buyer with the most to gain from acquisition of the divested activity and adroit negotiating are the ingredients of an optimum divestment agreement.

Tailoring the Divestment Package

The initial determination to divest includes a description of what is to be divested from the viewpoint of the divesting company alone.

Crucible Steel wants to rid itself of its West Virginia coal mine properties.

Du Pont wants to withdraw from its Corfam operations.

Schlitz want to sell its Brooklyn brewery.

What makes sense as a divestment may have no particular relation to what makes sense as an acquisition, nor need it relate to a specific stream of benefit flow from the activity divested. The divesting company can assess its bargaining position and modify its divestment entity if it understands the prospective purchaser's unique requirements. Minimally, the divesting company can assess the importance of possible modifications to the divestment entity during the give and take of divestment negotiations.

Product lines and production capability may be treated separately. The buyer may need additional manufacturing capacity but not be able to fit the divested activity's product line into its own distribution system easily. Or the buyer may seek the divested activity's market position but possess more than sufficient production capability.

American Zinc Company had closed its refinery at Sauget, Illinois. Subsequently, American Metal Climax evidenced interest because of a possible need for the available plant capacity.

Particular benefits may be realized by a prospective purchaser from operations in one geographic area. Geographic separation and divestment activity may be advantageous to the buyer.

The ten snack food plants to be divested by Frito-Lay were all centrally located except for one plant in the Pacific Northwest. At one point in the negotiations a divestment agreement could have satisfied many of the company's divestment objectives except that it would have excluded the single plant on the West Coast.

The attractiveness of some divested activities may lie solely in certain held rights, patents, manufacturing practices, or contracts. Remaining assets may have value to the buyer only through their liquidation, which might also hold true for the divesting company that finds only its key elements wanted.

The Du Pont sale of its Corfam operation to a Polish group consisted essentially of the technology along with an agreement to design and assist in the construction of a plant in Poland.

The question of tailoring the divestment entity is most evident when companies such as Boise Cascade, Whittaker, Penn Central, and American Standard (N.Y.) embark on large-scale divestment programs; the companies are seeking to divest for reasons other than the specifics of the divested activity itself. Considerable flexibility in constructing a divestment agreement is possible if the divesting company is prepared to negotiate creatively.

NINE

The Divestment Package

THIS CHAPTER deals with the divestment package itself. Particular attention is given to the form of the purchase—cash, notes, stock, exchange, or some combination of those elements. Also, the method of payment is discussed—immediacy versus over time and with or without contingencies. In advance of the discussion of those two issues, it bears repeating that the needs and objectives of both the divesting company and the prospective purchaser must be thoroughly understood if an optimum or merely a successful divestment is to be achieved. It is also important that the divesting company understand the points on which it can most easily give ground and on which a buyer might be expected to compromise.

Form of the Divestment

The benefits to the divesting company fall into two broad categories. The first is the stream of benefits that result from no longer being tied to the divested activity. Included in that category are the elimination of operating losses and the avoidance of future resource commitments. Those benefits were discussed in preceding chapters. No further comment is needed except that such benefits are not inconsequential and ordinarily accrue only to the divesting

Table 12. Form of divestment.

FORM	PERCENT REPLYING
Only cash	59
Cash and other forms	33
Never cash	8

company; they are not a matter of give and take with a prospective purchaser.

The second category of benefits includes the forms of payment. In the survey of corporate divestment practices, cash was most frequently cited as the form preferred (Table 12). Fewer than one out of ten firms responding to a question about form of payment indicated that cash was not wanted, and a closer look at those respondents revealed that in almost every case some form of exchange made these divestments atypical transactions. However, each payment form has its advantages and disadvantages that are relative to the circumstances of the divesting company and the prospective purchaser.

Cash

Cash has the special advantages of certainty and definiteness. Not even notes have those characteristics if the viability of the purchaser is questionable.

In acquisitions during the late 1960s by such companies as Boise Cascade, Penn Central, and National Student Marketing Corp., the use of notes could have created subsequent problems for the divesting company. Cash payment would have avoided any difficulty.

Notes

Notes most closely approach the certainty and definiteness of cash. The reason, of course, is their direct convertibility into cash, assuming the notes are redeemed as stipulated. A special case occurs when the prospective purchaser is a foreign government. Notes are the most usual foreign government payment form, and the uncertainty over their redemption is high. Also, if payment is to be made in the currency of the buying country, the valuation may be substantially impaired by currency exchange losses.

When payment is in the form of either cash or notes, however, contingent payments could negate the certainty and definiteness. Contingent payments are discussed later in this chapter.

Stock

Purchases with stock usually involve the securities of the buying company, and here uncertainty rather than certainty prevails. Stock purchases introduce a wide range of problems related to immediacy, liquidity, and convertibility.

A stock purchase may not provide the divesting company with immediate resources that it can utilize to reduce its own debt burden or commit to any of its other undertakings. The stock used in the divestment purchase may be unlisted, or there may be restrictions on its use. Subsequently, when the restrictions no longer apply, trading in the stock may reduce the ease of liquidity. The divesting company may find that it can convert to cash only gradually. Finally, fluctuating stock market values along with uncertainty over the future strength of the purchasing company could reduce the likelihood of eventual convertibility of the stock into equivalent cash value.

A sale to employees has all of the potential hazards of purchase with stock. The result may be that a private company prevents any immediate use of the stock by the divesting company, and the uncertainty over the eventual public stock trading raises a question of ultimate liquidity.

The risks of failure that confront the new company make convertibility into equivalent cash at least doubtful.

Payment in stock offers two advantages. First, tax benefits can be created through a tax-free stock exchange. However, in a divestment as opposed to a typical acquisition, the seller is more apt to be accounting for a loss than a gain. Nonetheless, the consideration should be kept in mind by the divesting company.

The second advantage is that the stock may appreciate in value. Of course, it could also depreciate. However, if the divested activity is expected to have a substantial favorable effect on the price of the buying company's stock and if that effect seems probable because of the positive circumstances into which the divested activity will be put, payment in stock could be advantageous to the divesting company.

TRW Inc. sold its Hazelton Laboratories subsidiary to Environmental Science Corp. in part for convertible preferred stock. Environmental Sciences provides equipment for the care of laboratory animals; Hazelton engages in independent laboratory testing and cancer research. The combination might be expected by TRW to have a positive impact on the future price of the stock.

Exchange

The exchange is an infrequently used form of purchase. It is not always clear in exchange transactions whether the divesting company is actually anxious to divest or is really interested in what is obtained by the exchange. The divestment of hotel properties occasionally takes place by exchange.

National Realty Investors divested its Dinkler-Plaza Hotel in Atlanta by exchanging it for the Sahara Club apartments in suburban Atlanta.

Combinations

Divestment purchases need not be limited to any single one of the payment forms but may instead be made by some combination of them. Some cash may be included to meet the minimum resource needs of the divesting company but lie within the cash payment ability of the purchaser. Notes can be added to the extent of some minimum acceptable valuation. Stock may be included to compensate the divesting company for accepting a small amount of cash at the time of the agreement.

Divestment Payment Method

The divestment package must define not only the form of payment but also the conditions of the payment.

Payment Timing

The divesting and purchasing companies are at opposite corners on the timing of the purchase payment. To the divesting firm, receiving full value immediately is preferable, particularly if the divestment has been prompted by a need for resources. To the purchasing firm, stretched-out payments with a nominal amount in the beginning is preferable, for that means conserving resources and hopefully obtaining the balance from the earnings of the divested activity.

The divestment acquisition differs significantly from other acquisitions in the subsequent status of the seller. In many acquisitions, the former owners remain to manage the business, and so some formula of payment over time can be agreed upon to the mutual benefit and security of buyer and seller. In a divestment, the selling company typically is no longer involved with the operation of the activity and no longer has the security of firsthand control.

Valuation is usually related to payment timing: the prompter the payment, the lower the valuation. In some situations, however, stretching out the payments may be agreed upon as the best if not the only way to reach a consensus on valuation. As an example, the possible future value of the divested activity may bear no resemblance to any historical performance that might be used as a basis for current price or valuation. The prospective purchaser might be interested in expectations but be unwilling to correlate immediate payment with expected but uncertain future performance. The divesting company, on the other hand, might be willing to forego a lower, immediate payment because of its confidence that a payment formula based on future performance promises a substantially greater recovery.

RCA divested its customer base to Sperry Rand for about $70 million in cash plus contingent sums that could total $30 to $60 million over a five-year period.

The advantage in such arrangements would seem to lie with the buying company. It defers the use of its own resources and has control over the future performance base. As for the divesting company, not only is its recovery of resources deferred but future payments are beyond its jurisdiction.

Payment Contingencies

Payment may not only be stretched out over a period of years but may also be made dependent on such future conditions as the performance of the divested activity. Those conditions differ from the ordinary legal representations included in an agreement because they are primarily of a business rather than a legal nature. Future profits or sales levels are the most typical contingent conditions, but others also may be part of the divestment agreement.

During Crucible Steel's negotiations on the divestment of its coal properties, a provision to tie payments to future coal prices was proposed.

It is the buying company that will seek to include protective clauses in the divestment agreement. When the divesting company finds that it must accept such clauses, it should look to higher valuation and an improvement in the payment terms as compensation.

In summary, the divestment package represents the agreed-upon compromise between the objectives and requirements of the divesting firm and those of the purchaser. Table 13 summarizes the two positions. To a great extent,

Table 13. Divestment package preferences.

	DIVESTOR	PURCHASER
Form	Cash	Stock
	Notes	
Method	Now	Future

the elements can be interchanged with or without changes in valuation. Again, only if the divesting company understands both its own and the buyer's positions can trade-offs maximize the benefits to the divestor.

TEN

Communicating
the Divestment Action

ONCE THE DIVESTMENT AGREEMENT has been negotiated and signed, implementation begins. It requires communication.

The communication question is no longer whether to communicate, since the transaction is now public knowledge. At this point, if some kind of preliminary announcement was not made, communication must accommodate a possible adverse shock effect of the completion of the divestment.

How and with whom to communicate are discussed here. The communication must reach the many constituencies of the divesting company—stockholders, employees, customers, and suppliers—as well as the general public.

Stockholders

The divesting company's stockholders are concerned with the economic well-being of their company. They need to know what short- and long-term impact the divestment action will have on the company's future profit performance. That information may have to be imparted to them when management credibility is in doubt.

The credibility difficulty arises because the stockholders may not have realized there was any reason for concern about the activity divested. In fact, whatever information had been released to them previously might well have described the activity very positively. If trouble had been noted, it would probably have been in connection with turning the situation around. Furthermore, it is not unusual, especially among multi-industry firms, for the divestment to be of a former acquisition. In total, not only might the stockholders have been unaware of the true critical state of the activity but they may now find a substantial disparity between the amount paid for the acquisition, once explained to them in glowing terms, and the divestment price.

It is important that the divesting company's stockholders leave after the announcement with the feeling that management is presently in full control of the situation, whatever mistakes may have led to the need to divest. Thus it may be essential to restate the objectives and assumptions that governed the company's initial participation in the activity and to explain the changes in conditions that have caused management to divest.

A major food company entered the manufacture of synthetic sweeteners. At the time of entry, demand for the product was projected to more than double, supply was severely strained, and prices were extremely high. As events unfolded in the ensuing several years, low-calorie sweeteners for food, as distinct from soft drinks, never developed as anticipated. Supply, on the other hand, increased dramatically, and that resulted in a precipitous price decline to less than one-third the earlier price level. Substantial losses in the operation forced the company to end its involvement in that market.

Stockholders must be convinced that management is cognizant of the conditions responsible for the present situation. Furthermore, they must believe that management is now correct in its decision to divest at the announced terms. They must overcome any prejudice arising from earlier management decisions and actions that have proved to be in error. Candor is more likely to be the better part of valor.

Employees

Communication with the employees of the divesting company, particularly those of the divested activity, is especially critical. The workers may already be reacting adversely to the many rumors that are rife during such periods. Employees are understandably concerned about job security, future benefits, and remaining opportunities. For that reason, communication with the employees of the divested activity should be drafted in coordination with the purchasing company. It is essential that the information from the two companies be consistent, especially as it relates to the jobs of the employees. Much of a positive nature about the renewed and increased support for the activity expected from the new owners can be said. The message to be imparted to the workers is that the dilemma faced by the divesting company has been resolved, or at least is being acted upon, by the new owners.

Divestments by financially troubled Beck Industries were made when Beck itself was in bankruptcy. Offers to purchase segments of the distressed company were made almost daily. The employees could not be blamed if they were preoccupied with their job future.

The first priority, then, is to stress the viability of the divested activity in the hands of the new owners. To some extent, the explanation may require emphasis on what the new owners will do with the divested activity that the former owners were unable or unwilling to do.

Once the essential viability of the activity has been established, attention should be directed toward the specifics about the employees' jobs: whether the jobs will continue to exist and what changes will be made in them under new owners and perhaps new management. The employees would like truthful answers to a few questions:

1. Is the job going to be eliminated?
2. Is the job content going to be changed?
3. Will the job be moved geographically?
4. Is the union contract, if any, to remain in force?
5. Are the various pension or insurance rights to be upheld?

The list could be extended, but its point is that the employees have a right to know what may happen to their jobs. For the sake of both the divesting and the buying companies, the employees must be reassured if performance of the divested activity is to be maintained and improved.

To be avoided in communications to employees are categorical statements about business activity or job security that company officials know to be of questionable validity. Initial statements that prove false can do much to undermine a successful takeover.

Remaining Employees

As to the divesting company's remaining employees, the substance and handling of the divestment communication will make a very deep impression on them. If there is a possibility that other activities of the divesting company might be sold, the employees associated with those operations will be most alert to how employees of the divested activity were treated. Their work performance will reflect their concern.

The divesting company should inform all its employees as briefly and as clearly as possible of the conditions that brought about the divestment. It should explain how the divestment relates to other company activities. More will be said about employee relations in the following chapter.

Business Relationships

Customers and suppliers look upon the divestment from the viewpoint of how the action might affect their business relationships with the divested activity. Although divestment generally means the continuation of the divested operations and therefore the need to maintain the divested activity's customer and supplier relationships, both customers and suppliers will be looking for affirmation of existing associations.

Customers

The customers' concern is a continued source of supply. The new owner might eliminate or trim back some of the product line and thereby affect the customers' purchase plans, or it might initiate revised pricing or discount policies that could cause the customers to reevaluate their sources of supply. Even changes in production scheduling or transfers of production from one plant to another could cause concern among the customers.

Those observations are not meant to suggest that the customers of the divested activity will necessarily find the changes, if and when they are introduced, to be disadvantageous. More vigorous support could very possibly make the divested activity a far more attractive source of supply.

As for the divesting company proper, if it expects to continue selling to the same customers from its remaining operations, it should be solicitous that its continuing relationship with them is not jeopardized by mishandling of the communication phase of the divestment implementation.

At least, the divesting company can make sure that neither misinformation or lack of information is at fault.

Suppliers

Suppliers may find that their status with the divested activity is affected by relations between the new owners and other suppliers. They could, in other words, find themselves without that customer. On the other hand, the divestment could work to their advantage. Through their relation with the divested activity, they could gain entry to a new and substantial customer, the new owner.

To the divesting company itself and its remaining operations, future relations with the suppliers could be a concern. Pricing, credit terms, and shipment schedules to the remaining segments of the company from some of its suppliers may have been predicated upon or influenced greatly by the volume of purchases from the divested activity. The divesting company must make an immediate effort to communicate to those suppliers what is happening, if for no other reason than to maintain an atmosphere of mutual trust.

The Public

Finally, the divesting company has a public image that requires attention. Its public includes, very importantly, the community in which the divested activity has facilities or offices. To that immediate public, the most essential information will concern the employees living and working in the community. Beyond information on how those employees are treated, the community will be concerned about the future vitality of the business within its borders. That is of great importance when the divested activity is a major employer and taxpayer. Furthermore, if officials of the divested activity have played an active role as civic leaders of the community, the continuation of that civic contribution will be questioned.

How communication of the divestment is handled will form the basis for general public judgment of how well the divesting company has managed one of its major corporate problems. A suggestion of bafflement or inability to solve the problems of the divested activity may have left an unfavorable impression. The way the divesting company handles the divestment can restore its image of competence and decisiveness.

ELEVEN

Divestment
and the Employees

SPECIAL ATTENTION should be given to the employees because of the potential impact of the divestment on their jobs. Divestment is a business decision and as such is impersonal, but loss of or change in jobs is a decidedly personal matter for the employees.

Management

Management of the divested activity is a distinctly unique and varied problem. Because its status following divestment depends entirely on the special conditions of that operation, the treatment of management can be seen to vary widely. Sometimes the management turns out to be the new owners, the purchasing group. If the divested activity's managers have assumed that position, they clearly have defined their roles in the postdivestment situation.

International Utilities Corp. sold its Bradford-White Corp. subsidiary to the activity management. The president and executive vice president retained their positions.

Even when the divested activity's management is not part of the purchasing group, its future role may be intrinsic to the divestment. The buying group may regard a commitment of its continued involvement as essential if the divested activity is to contribute to its own operations.

Doric Corp. bought the Patterson Dental Co. unit of the Sybron Corp. to provide it with entry into the rapidly developing dental equipment and supply business. The retention of Patterson's management team was essential to the success of Doric's entry.

The reverse of the preceding set of conditions may exist. The buyers may view the unit's current management as part of the problem engulfing the activity and seek to remove it as soon as possible.

A private group sought to purchase a large retail furniture and appliance division of a financial services company. The division had lost money over the preceding several years and had closed down a number of its retail units. The new owners intended to take over direct operation of the division and replace many of its key management people in an effort to shake up the company and get it moving again.

Finally, the divesting company, or even the purchasing company for that matter, may wish to draw upon the management of the divested activity much as it would a general management pool. That, however, is more likely to be true of a shutdown rather than a divestment.

Time Inc. used the demise of *Life* magazine as an opportunity to transfer some of the key members of management into other Time enterprises and occasionally even to replace current management.

To a question about special separation arrangements for the management of the divested activity, nearly two-thirds of the company respondents indicated that they did make such arrangements. Often the special treatment might require the full knowledge and cooperation of the purchaser, particularly if the purchaser is to be dependent on the management group for the success of its acquisition.

A case in point is the IBM divestment of its service bureau and time-sharing operations to Control Data Corp. The example is unique only in the extent of the special arrangements necessary to satisfy the key personnel of the divested activity in their changeover under Control Data. Items such as IBM stock holdings and retirement provisions needed special handling to resolve the differences between the IBM and Control Data programs.

As can be seen from a few examples, generalizations about the handling of divested company management personnel are difficult or impossible to make. The first essential is knowledge of whether the personnel are to stay with the divested activity or with the divesting company. Once that is known, questions of contracts, stock options, special fringe benefits, and so on can be fitted into the context of the individual role.

Employees

The impact of divestment on the employees of a divested activity can range from quite minimal to very substantial. If the divested operation continues to function in much the same way, employees may notice little if any effect of the divestment. Existing management may continue in charge; the same customer and supplier relationships may be maintained; the labor contract may be unchanged in regard to wage, fringe benefit, and working provisions; and even the divested activity's name may be the same.

The Ivy Hill Lithograph Corp. bought the assets of the Ivy Hill Lithograph division of the Whittaker Corp. Ivy Hill, formed by the founders and former owners, continued its operations under the same management at both its eastern facility in Great Neck and its western plant in Los Angeles.

Conversely, the divestment might bring with its substantial changes including the shutdown or transfer of part of the operations. No labor contract may exist, which will permit widespread changes in working conditions and compensation arrangements. Under some circumstances new owners are unlikely to have concluded their acquisition of the divestment without feeling assured of a relatively free hand to introduce the policies and procedures they consider necessary for the turnaround of the operation. Then the objective in the treatment of the employees of the divested activity is to induce them to accept the changes.

Several things can be done to encourage effective employee participation in the changeover. The first lies in the framework of communications to employees, as discussed in the preceding chapter. Minimally, the employees deserve full knowledge of the new direction to be taken by the activity. Individual employees may not want to continue, which is their choice. If part of the divested activity's operation is to be shut down or relocated, if work assignments in the divested activity are to be modified, or if compensation agreements are to be changed, the employees should be informed so they can respond as soon as possible.

Second, the current employees should be given the first opportunity to continue with the divested activity. If part of the activity is to be relocated, some provision for transferring the employees who are willing to move should be made. If job assignments are to be changed, the current employees should be offered the training necessary to adjust to the changes. Existing employees can be given a chance even when the new owner intends, with good reason, to shake up the activity once it has gained control.

Finally, some employees just will not fit into the revised operations, though they might have wanted to. Even so, they deserve consideration. Severance arrangements will vary with the intentions and the economic capabilities of the selling and buying companies. The point is that steps can be taken, as part of the divestment implementation, to ease severance. Either or both companies should enlist government and private agencies to assist separated employees in their job searches. Both companies should give the separated employees job priority in their other operations.

The successful implementation of a divestment may reflect only marginally any extra consideration given to the employees of the divested activity, but the reason for concern lies beyond immediate gain. Concern for employees should not be constrained by prevailing work conditions or compensation arrangements, nor does a need to initiate changes exclude constructive obligation toward the employees affected by the changes.

Unions

Divestment has much the same impact on the union as on the employee. Note that the discussion of employee treatment recognized the union aspect of employment. But there is one aspect of union involvement that has not yet been mentioned. Union leadership could play a positive role in the handling of changes, particularly personnel and work changes, in connection with the implementation of the divestment. That thought is not universal. In fact, in the survey of corporate divestment practices no company indicated that it even considered participation of union leaders at any point in the divestment process.

Noninvolvement of union leadership in divestment activities is disconcerting. Many divestment problems would lend themselves to the cooperative efforts of everyone connected with the activity. Specifically, union leadership participation might be advantageous in resolving these tasks:

1. Part of the divested company operations may have to be shut down or relocated. Union leadership cooperation, or at least neutrality, would be most helpful.
2. Workers must be persuaded to accept changes in work assignments. Union leaders could assist and encourage those workers rather than attempt to undermine the job-restructuring effort.
3. Some employees may need retraining and perhaps new jobs outside the divested activity. Union leaders could be a helpful force in such retraining or reemployment.

A union will not go away and cannot be ignored. It is true that the concern of union leadership as it relates to union employees will often be quite different from the concern of the companies involved, but it is not unknown for union leadership, if and when it is permitted a meaningful role, to seek means of accommodation. There may be situations in which attempts at cooperation are doomed to failure, but on balance such attempts are worth the effort.

TWELVE

Implementing the Divestment

COMPLETION AND SIGNING of the divestment agreement is not the end of the divestment process; instead, it leads into the equally important implementation phase. In part, the importance of implementation may reflect certain requirements set by the divestment agreement. For example, the agreement may include contingencies related to the future performance of the divested activity that could affect the valuation ultimately paid or even the finality of the divestment itself.

Beyond its importance to the successful conclusion of the divestment and the treatment of the employees involved, implementation affects numerous relationships and raises issues that are central to the functioning of the divested activity and the divesting company. Among those covered in this chapter are customer relationships, supplier contracts, advertising and promotion programs, distribution arrangements, intracompany transactions, bond and other debt provisions, pension and insurance requirements, research programs, patent rights, and financial reporting adjustments.

The point of view taken in this chapter is that of the divesting company, although many of the considerations bear on the purchaser as well. To some extent, the points discussed can be included explicitly in the divestment agreement; and when that is possible, they should be. But for the most part, the subject of this chapter is how the divesting company reorders its remaining operations as it moves beyond the divestment.

Customer Relations

Customers of the divested activity are presumably to be retained, and the problem of retention faces both the divested activity and the purchaser. For them the difficulties that could arise include competition with the divesting company, especially if divestment was prompted by government antitrust action. Here, however, the discussion focuses on the remaining operations of the divesting company itself.

The divesting company may have important customers that buy various of its products and services from a number of its operations including the divested activity. Concern centers on those customers that looked upon their orders to the divested activity as the key to keeping most of the rest of their purchases with the other operations of the divesting company. A problem that might then arise is how the divesting company should handle pricing and service concessions that were based on a substantial volume of purchases from the divested activity.

Another problem in customer relations may arise from the uncertainty introduced by the divestment. Customers for products of other operations of the divesting company may become worried that further divestments will take place and jeopardize their source of supply. At the least, they may develop alternative supply sources or shift the proportions of their orders away from the divesting company. In either case, the divesting company will suffer a loss in sales.

The divesting company must understand the possibility

and potentiality of those responses. It can and must take steps to counteract the adverse influence of the divestment action on its customers. First, of course, comes sound and effective communications with the customers. Even if other divestments are under review, the divesting company must strive to maintain its credibility as a supplier. Candor could have negative repercussions at a later date, but anything less than candor with major customers could result in inconvenience or even losses to them and so risk their alienation.

Besides formal communications, the divesting company should establish a special customer relations effort aimed directly at each important customer affected by the divestment. Preferably, the contacts should be between key personnel of both the divesting company and the customer. At the minimum, questions in the customer's mind can be answered. Perhaps the inclination to cut back on purchases from other divesting company operations can be reversed. The customer is the focus of the business, and no effort should be spared to shore up relationships that are certain to be weakened by the divestment action.

Suppliers

The obligations specified in supplier contracts with the divested activity are ordinarily covered in the divestment agreement. The purchaser usually assumes the fulfillment of contractual obligations. As for the divesting company, any concern may be over the relations between such suppliers and the remaining company operations. Especially if the divested activity was a major purchaser from a particular supplier, such considerations as pricing, payment terms, and delivery schedules may affect the divesting company's other orders.

Accordingly, the divesting company should carefully

review its supplier relations. Its purchasing department may have to do some strenuous renegotiating to preserve current advantages. Some supplier changes may also result from the review.

Advertising and Promotion

Specific advertising and promotional material, as well as certain media commitments, may be taken over in total by the purchaser as part of the divestment agreement. Cancellation by the divesting company of some advertising efforts may also have been agreed upon.

The problem for the divesting company is that discussed in connection with suppliers: media and other advertising pricing for all of the divesting company's business may have been predicated on the orders generated by the divested activity. Another problem could arise if advertising and promotion of the divested activity's products or services was included in general advertising and promotional efforts. The reverse situation is also possible: the advertising and promotion of the divesting company's other product lines may have revolved around that of the divested activity.

Divestment necessitates a review of the overall advertising and promotion effort in order to delete references to the divested activity as well as to reinforce support for remaining product lines. The latter may be somewhat orphaned by the divestment and in a position to suffer by the elimination of advertising and promotion centered on the divested activity.

Distributors

The divested activity will, at least in the beginning, doubtless continue to utilize its existing distributor arrangements. The divesting company, however, may have a problem with distributors that have been supporting its other products because of the business brought them by the divested activity. The divesting company could experience waning distributor support for its remaining products.

Divestment therefore requires a careful examination of the distribution system. The divesting company may have to concentrate its remaining business with fewer distributors to secure needed support, or it may have to develop new distributor arrangements. The problem is never explicitly raised, but unless the divesting company pays close heed to the effect the divestment might have had on its distributors, it will experience declining sales. The concern could be even more pointed if the purchaser should have other products that it could persuade the distributors to support ahead of the divesting company's products.

Intracompany Transactions

Dealings between the company and its divested activity can pose a wide range of difficulties. The profitability of some remaining company operations could have been dependent on favorable treatment accorded by the divested activity. For example, intracompany transfers of product at cost instead of selling price could have made the cost of goods to subsequent operations unrealistically low. The absorption of certain costs attendant on various services rendered by the divested activity, favorable treatment on goods returned to the divested activity, special production runs, and the holding of inventory are some of the possible special arrangements between sister operations. It is unlikely that the purchaser will continue such support.

Divestment should force a review of all intracompany transactions. Hopefully, such transactions have been recognized in the divestment agreement; analysis of them could point up some disturbing ramifications of the kind described in the preceding paragraph. Also, the special arrangements could hinge on the divested activity being a customer of other divesting company operations. The divested activity might take products that could not be shipped to other customers, correct defects in shipments received rather than return the goods, or pay more promptly than other customers. Even the substantial order volume that might have been provided by the intracompany customer could be crucial to the divesting company's operations and pricing.

As stated, much of the intracompany question could and should have been resolved within the divestment agreement, at least on the points of any significance. More importantly, from the standpoint of the divesting company, the issues raised by the intracompany transactions should have been identified, analyzed, and resolved as part of the analytical process that led to the divestment decision.

Bonds and Other Debts

Legal constraints tied into previous borrowings by the divesting company might affect the sale of company assets or operations. Those constraints may impose limitations on both the valuation acceptable or the method of payment suitable. Furthermore, the use of the divestment proceeds in relation to debt retirement probably will be proscribed.

Bond or debt restrictions are of particular importance because access to those proceeds could have been one of the compelling reasons for divestment. On the other hand, the use of divestment proceeds for debt retirement could result in the removal of capital constraints that had been preventing the divesting company from undertaking certain new programs. Bond and debt considerations should have been carefully examined as part of the divestment decision analysis.

Pensions and Insurance

The divesting company must exercise care that, when it completes the divestment, it is not left with obligations to various pension funds or liabilities under certain insurance contracts. Pension and insurance obligations should be covered explicitly in the divestment agreement; frequently, they are part of a labor contract that the purchaser should be expected to assume.

Questions that should be resolved include unfunded payments to retirees of the divested activity, commitments to bring unfunded pensions to a satisfactory and actuarially sound level, and claims against the divested activity for use of joint facilities that were either self-insured or only partially insured by the divesting company. No attempt is made here to be definitive about possible sleeper situations in the pension and insurance areas. It is incumbent on the divesting company to obtain the necessary professional review of those items to diminish the possibility of later and unknown liabilities. Probably such a review will have to be undertaken anyway because of demands by the purchaser for such information.

Research

Research activities of the divesting company may not be segregated among the operating units. However, overall support of research may be tied to total sales volume, which will be reduced by the divestment. Also, some research programs may have been directly or indirectly intended for the divested activity. The overall research program of the divested company should therefore be reevaluated against the needs of the remaining operations. Some projects might have to be curtailed or eliminated, whereas others might receive renewed emphasis.

One aspect of the divestment negotiation is the value of research programs and their support that could be added to the divestment package. Research facilities and equipment might also add to the valuation. Whenever possible, decisions on such inclusions should be made before entering the divestment negotiations.

Patents

Patents related directly to the divested activity's operations are likely to be included specifically in the divestment agreement. If patents cover products or processes used elsewhere within the remaining operations of the divesting company, a separate understanding or agreement will be required. What must be avoided is the transfer of patents or of rights to them in the absence of arrangements for access if and when it is needed.

In many respects, patents and research programs are related. The usefulness of either one to the divesting company may diminish considerably following the divestment; yet for some purposes the patents could be integral with remaining operations. Since research programs and even patents are often of unknown value, their unintentional omission from the divestment agreement is not difficult.

Financial Reporting

The divesting company has no legal or accounting obligation to segregate the divested activity from remaining company activities in the data used and presented. Yet, as in an acquisition, inclusion of the divested activity in the historical data of the company doing the divesting does distort forward comparisons and analyses of the divesting company's performance. At least for internal control purposes, adjustments to the company's data base should be made to isolate the divested activity from past information.

THIRTEEN

Divestment as an Opportunity

CERTAIN FORCES at work within the business community are making divestments an increasingly important consideration. The purpose of this book has been to explore management techniques for handling situations in which divestment is at least an alternative approach. Prerequisite to the use of the technique, however, is a set of rational attitudes toward divestment.

Divestment is becoming a more frequent business occurrence. Divestment is being talked of more often because it is happening more often. Quantitative data are scarce and somewhat incomplete, but the information that is available points unmistakably to a rising incidence. Divestments now represent perhaps one-third of current acquisitions and have been doubling and redoubling every few years over the past decade or two.

Behind the growing divestment frequency are certain fundamental forces that will accelerate the trend. First, the changes in corporate reporting, particularly those that require reporting by segment of company business, will focus attention on company activities that are not up to company standards. Management is thus more likely to be forced into positions in which divestment must at least be considered. Second, inclusion of divestment review in the organized planning process will result in company trouble spots being examined repeatedly and systematically. The divestment alternative will be compared with other possible responses to the situation. Third, the very fact of increasing frequency has given divestment an element of respectability that had been missing.

Divestment should be regarded as a normal part of business life. Divestment should be viewed as one of many responses to a growing, changing, dynamic business world. The increasing frequency of divestment should be viewed not as an aberration but as a normal consequence of certain basic forces at work. Among those forces are the life cycle processes: through a quite normal course of events, a product, activity, or unit outlives its initial usefulness and should be shed. Also included is the human factor, which surfaces in mistaken business judgments of products, activities, or methods. Finally there is the dynamism of the company that grows, changes, and finds itself no longer needing involvements that were previously most important to it.

Divestment should be considered as only one of many company responses to a situation. Divestment should not be an isolated consideration; it should evolve from an organized response to a company situation. Alternatives include shutdown, changes in price structure, cost reduction, new product introduction, and change in operating management. In the context, divestment, although not the only response, is most likely the final response.

Essential to analysis and evaluation of the alternatives is a system that can provide information on the causes of the situation. Something more than knowledge that profits are inadequate or sales are lagging is needed; the company must know why. The underlying cause may be technological obsolescence, changes in consumer buying tastes, or rise in cost of raw materials, but only when the true nature of the problem is known can the divestment decision be part of a total approach to company management.

Divestment requires organizational responsibility. A necessary corollary to the axiom that divestment is only one of an array of responses to company situations is that divestment must be a specific organizational responsibility. As has been noted, it is most appropriately included in the planning process, and therefore the planning group should have responsibility for its regular inclusion in company review. The managers directly involved in the activity that may be divested should participate; they contribute to an understanding of the consequences of the possible alternative courses of action.

Search for and approach to prospective purchasers should be organized, not left to chance. Once the decision to divest is made, an orderly and systematic search for a buyer should be undertaken. To that end, the objective of the divestment should be clear: to unload an unprofitable activity, to obtain additional financial resources, to comply with a government antitrust action. The established objective will guide the search for a purchaser. Further, it can be an invaluable guide in the approach to the prospective purchaser, for it should enable the divesting company to tailor its contact to evoke a positive response.

All that is little different from the intelligent pursuit of an acquisition program. An effective acquisition program focuses on specific companies within specific industries or markets. Also, the initial contact of those companies rests on an understanding of what might prompt a favorable reply. A divestment is really just a reverse acquisition.

Candor rather than secrecy is advisable. One of the more controversial aspects of divestment is the question of candor versus secrecy. The specific reference is usually to early contacts with prospective purchasers, but it can apply to information provided the management and employees of the activity to be divested and to suppliers, customers, stockholders, and the public as well. No doubt there are occasions on which short-term or even long-term advantage has been secured through secrecy. The argument for candor reflects a belief that an aura of mutual trust can thereby be generated and that such trust is essential to the ultimate signing of a divestment agreement. It can also be argued that candor in dealings with employees, suppliers, customers, stockholders, and the public is the foundation of a long-term relationship that is in the best interests of the divesting company.

That is not to say that the company should not place its difficulties in a positive light. But acknowledging that they exist and are being reacted to may well speak more favorably for the company than secrecy would, for the other parties are frequently aware that something is amiss. Their imagination, if unchecked, will probably be more damaging to the divesting company than the actual facts. Too often, failure to disclose reflects management's unwillingness to face some of the unpleasant aspects of the situation.

Divestment ends with the implementation, not with the agreement. Much that is written of an acquisition ends with the signing of the divestment agreement, but critical aspects of the total transaction follow that signing. Not the least of them is the communication of the divestment agreement to the many parties concerned. It is essential that the divesting company consider its future relations with all interested parties and position itself with them as favorably as possible through the communication.

Also necessary is proper handling of the employees directly involved with the divestment. That handling, important in itself in respect to equity of treatment, will be assessed by employees elsewhere in the divesting company. The impact on employee morale and the response to that impact can be of critical importance to the divesting company.

Divestment need not be catastrophic. Perhaps the central theme of this book is that divestment should be approached as an opportunity and not as a disaster. Difficulties abound, and an optimum divestment is not overly easy to accomplish. Yet divestment ought to be viewed as a chance to turn a less than favorable situation into a future benefit to the divesting company. At the least, divestment can be withdrawal from an unfavorable situation. More positively, it can provide financial resources for existing or new undertakings and, equally important, it can free managerial attention and effort and direct it toward other opportunities. Finally, the willingness to make such a wrenching decision can have an overall beneficial impact on the entire company. Divestment is no less traumatic than it ever was, but it can and should be accepted within the framework of actions that are taken because they are best for the future course of the company.

APPENDIX

Questions Used in This Survey

1. Does your company have a means, formal or informal, for reviewing its activities to identify possibilities for divestment: a division, a product line, a facility, a technological position?

2. How would or does your company define divestment and what type of divestment falls under or is included within this definition in your company?

3. If the divestment review function exists within your company, how is this function organized?

    (a) A specific person has been assigned or a particular department has been established with this function as its sole or at least primary responsibility.

    (b) The responsibility for the performance of this divestment function has been given to a single person or department as one of its tasks or responsibilities.

    (c) The responsibility for the divestment function is diffused throughout the company, with no specific assignments designated, but the function exists within a management procedure such as regular profit planning reviews or exists within committees established in the company structure such as the finance committee.

4. Please provide specific titles and department descriptions concerned with divestment if such exist within your company.

5. Which of the following factors have been elements in any

of your company's divestment reviews or divestment decisions? (Frequently, occasionally, never.)

A change in the strategic plans or long-range objectives of the parent company or of the activity to be divested.

Antitrust rulings or charges or threats of antitrust rulings or charges.

Divestment process required as source of funds for debt retirement or as source for company expansion in other areas.

Activity to be divested requires resources beyond those that can be made available to it within the company or it requires a diversion of the company's resources that could be more effectively deployed in other activities.

Activity to be divested has had or is projected to have a harmful impact on company earnings or return on investment.

Parent company or activity to be divested is faced with constraints of market, distribution, or production.

Other (explain).

6. Does your company have a divestment policy—

As to activities and products to be considered or excluded from divestment evaluation and review?

As to specific criteria to be included in a divestment analysis and "standards" for making divestment decisions such as rate of return, share of market, rate of growth?

As to procedures or steps in the divestment evaluation and implementation?

7. What financial criteria are used in your company's divestment evaluations? (Check if yes.)

Sales

Growth in sales

Operating margins

Contribution to overhead

Return on total investment

Return on equity

Return on assets employed

Return on sales

Cash flow
Impact on costs of remaining products
Impact on revenues of remaining products
Breakeven analysis
Other (explain)

8. What time factors would or did bear on your divestment decision?

Labor contracts expiration
Negotiation of major customers and/or supplier contracts
Effective date for new regulatory controls
Commitment of capital funds
Other (explain)

9. What other alternatives are or have been considered when divestment has been a possibility? (Check if yes.)

Shut down
Continuing on as is
Milking the operation and then disposing of it
Addition of product or product line
Cost reduction program including cost-reducing capital improvements
Pricing review
New product introduction
Acquisition of advantageous manufacturing or distribution capability
Acquisition or merger with competitor, supplier, or customer
Other (explain)

10. How were potential divestment purchasers sought?

Analysis of companies in related fields (such as customers, competitors, or suppliers)
Direct contact of prospect
Banks
Accounting firms
Lawyers
Consultants
Investment bankers
Brokers

Advertising such as in the *Wall Street Journal*
Other leads (explain)

11. What forms did the divestment purchase take? If a combination, please rank in order of importance, with *1* for the most important and so forth.
    Cash
    Stock
    Payout
    Exchange
    Other (explain)

12. What criterion is used to determine the value of the divested activity?
    Earnings
    Book value
    Other (explain)

13. Where a divestment has taken place, how were personnel in the divested activity handled?

14. How and when was the news of the divestment issued?

15. When was the union, if any, involved?

16. Were any special separation arrangements established for personnel no longer needed or not desiring to stay?

17. Did the departure of the divested activity's personnel have any effect on any existing or proposed employee plans such as the following?
    Insurance
    Pensions
    Stock plans
    Vacations
    Sabbaticals

Index